HENRI LAMBERT :
A GREAT MILITANT FOR PEACE
(1913-1919)

AN ADVISOR TO COLONEL HOUSE
(INTIMATE FRIEND AND PRINCIPAL POLITICAL COUNSELOR
OF PRESIDENT WILSON)

D/2017/6126/1

Printed by ILLUSTRATA
B-8870 IZEGEM

Printed in Belgium

Pierre CASIMIR-LAMBERT

Henri Lambert :
a great militant for peace
(1913-1919)

An advisor to Colonel House
(intimate friend and principal political counselor
of President Wilson)

2017

Henri Lambert (1862-1934).

Colonel House in 1915 (1858-1938)

Summary

Introduction

This is a short description of the contacts which developed at the highest level between my Belgian grandfather, Henri Lambert and Colonel House, dating from the middle of World War I to the Armistice of 1918. I wish to relate and record Henri Lambert's little-known, unrelenting efforts to bring about an early end to the "Great War", and above all, to win over to his ideas the most important world leader of 1916 to 1920 – US President Woodrow Wilson – with the aim of achieving a sound and lasting peace.

As a prominent European and Belgian industrialist, economist, sociologist, reformer, and rational pacifist, Henri Lambert led his struggle to the very top of the world leadership as his relationship developed with Colonel House – the esteemed right-hand adviser of President Wilson on foreign affairs (1).

Henri Lambert had long fought for "Free Trade" and against the extreme protectionism of the principal rival industrial powers, as the 19th century ended and the 20th century began with rising international tensions.

Sensing the approaching catastrophe of a great European conflict, Henri Lambert in April 1913 launched a lengthy "open letter" to the British Foreign Secretary, Sir Edward Grey, on the fundamental and moral importance of opening up economic relations between rival nations. As a first step, he proposed that a Convention be drawn up and signed to at least gradually open up the economic relations of the colonies to each other.

This call was widely heard, but not listened to, let alone considered, as the "Sleepwalkers" (2) of 1913 to 1914 led the world to the great disaster.

---

(1) "The importance of Colonel Edward M. House is enormous from 1918 to 1919, he served not only as intimate friend and chief political advisor to President Wilson but also as national security advisor and senior diplomat". (p. 171). Hodgson (G.), Woodrow Wilson's right-hand - The Life of Colonel Edward M. House, Oxford, Yale University Press, 200 p.

(2) Christophe Clark, Allen Law /2012, Penguin Books 2013 – "The Sleepwalkers – how Europe went to war in 1914".

The war, as apprehended by Henri Lambert, having broken out in Europe in August 1914, Henri Lambert wrote a widely read further "open letter" to President Wilson in early October 1914, again underlying the fundamental importance of the economic cause of the war, in the hope of Wilson negotiating a Peace. To no avail, once again, especially as Woodrow Wilson who was elected President in 1912, was very involved in domestic political matters (anti-trust especially) and had suffered the grievous loss of his beloved ailing wife, Ellen, in August 1914.

Henri was able to take exile in England with his adolescent son Valentin from September 1914 to the autumn of 1916 (with a short interlude spent in neutral Holland during 1915).

Upon arriving in England, in early September 1914, Henri Lambert promptly approached the leaders of the English pacifist movement. As a discerning, highly informed, leading pacifist militant, he wrote numerous articles, pamphlets, had high level political contacts, and even drew up a joint comprehensive, detailed peace plan with a leading English Member of Parliament (MP). The plan foresaw in detail an ending to the War based on a proposal of general "economic disarmament" by the gradual dismantling of trade barriers between the belligerents.

To no avail ! Despairing of the top British political leadership, and with a low regard for the English prime minister, Baldwin (3), he then turned to the United States as his only hope, and entered into contact with Colonel House (through an introduction by the President of Stanford University), to try to influence President Wilson. Henri Lambert clearly had some reason to believe that an intervention by President Wilson might be well received by the German Social Democrats, at the least.

A very discreet relationship gradually developed between the two men, some by direct contact, but mostly by correspondence, with Colonel House increasingly open to the thesis of Henri Lambert for the ending of hostilities.

On April 2nd, 1917, the highly militaristic German government having launched total submarine warfare, the United States entered into war.

On January 8th 1918, President Wilson made a historic speech of world-wide resonance, proposing to base a Peace Plan on "14 Points". Henri Lambert had hoped to the last that, through the influence of Colonel House, the Peace Plan would be based on general "economic disarmament" as its foremost, explicit and basic, principal "Point 1".

---

(3) Letter from Henri Lambert of 25th April 2017 to Colonel House (Yale University Library).

President Wilson and Edward M. House (1915).

Henri Lambert in United Kingdom (1915-1916).

Several decades later, my father Valentin often recounted both to me and my sister, Jacqueline, the ongoing efforts of our grandfather, Henri. Valentin had witnessed the events and lived with his father through those years from 1915 to mid - 1918, first in England, then in the US, before he was conscripted for Belgian military service and returned to Europe to serve in the Belgian army in France.

That great hope was dashed. With the support of Colonel House, Henri had only succeeded in having it raised from a lowly "Point 11" position on the list of aims drawn up by the "Inquiry" for President Wilson to "Point 3". The disappointment of Henri, who had hoped it would be the very founding principle of the "Wilsonian" Peace Plan, was profound but still he persisted.

As the exhausted European belligerents fought on into the autumn, the German early summer offensive having failed, and with US military and logistic support steadily increasing, the German army was in retreat and Germany itself was on the verge of internal collapse and social chaos in late September 1918.

Early in October 1918, negotiations for an Armistice suddenly opened up, carried out almost entirely between the United States and the new German Social Democratic government. The recommendations and advice of Henri Lambert to Colonel House, both for Europe and beyond, for the final negotiations soon gained momentum remarkably, up to the Armistice of November 11th, 1918.

As historians have known since, but very few participants then realised (4), the following 1919 "Paris Peace Conference" ended in disarray, with severe global consequences to this day as a result of the subsequent, deeply faulted Versailles Peace Treaty of June 25th, 1919.

President Wilson, having unexpectedly broken with Colonel House at the Peace Conference, had then completely abandoned "Point 3" ! At this crucial time, he was obsessed by his overriding dream of a "League of Nations to end all wars" and so exhausted by his tour of the US to gain support for it that he suffered a stroke from which he would never recover. He had also been overwhelmed by the narrow-minded French and British objectives and under constant attack from his US political opponents.

Last but not least, he was also engaged in trying to run for a third term in the presidential election. In March 1921, his presidency expired and he retired, very sick, with his second wife to Washington D.C. where he died in early 1924.

_____

(4) Except for John Maynard Keynes, as a young economist of the British Delegation, and Jean Monnet, as a young economist of the French delegation.

In deep despair, Henri Lambert shortly foresaw the development of a new major conflict breaking out for the next generation, with ever rising European political and social extremisms, along a new and even graver path to disaster…

My grandfather passed away accidentally in 1934, still an active militant for his ideas and world views, which all his life he had sought so hard to promote.

Pierre CASIMIR-LAMBERT
(Grandson of Henri Lambert)

The family name was extended en 1924 in memory of Henry Lambert's father and grandfather

BIBLIOGRAPHY

- H. LAMBERT, *Pax Economica, La liberté des échanges internationaux, fondement nécessaire et suffisant de la Paix universelle et permanente*, Bruxelles-Paris, 1920.

- H. LAMBERT, *Le Nouveau Contrat Social ou l'Organisation de la Démocratie Individualiste*, Paris, 1920.

- H. LAMBERT, *Hypothèse sur l'Évolution physique et métaphysique de l'Énergie*, Bruxelles, 1935.

For the complete bibliography, cf. J.-L. VAN BELLE, *Henri Lambert, Un grand penseur toujours d'actualité (1862-1934). Maître de verrerie, Économiste, Sociologue, Grand réformateur, Philosophe, Visionnaire*, Braine-le-Château, 2010, p. 375-385.

Valentin Casimir Lambert (1899-1987).

I

Introduction to Colonel House

ST. ERMINS HOTEL,

ST. JAMES' PARK, S.W.

TELEPHONES:
VICTORIA 7120 9 LINES.
TELEGRAMS:
"ERMINITES, LONDON"

18·11/16.

Sir,

I take the liberty of
sending you a pamphlet entitled
„Un autre aspect de la question
européenne et une solution" With
its English translation under the
title „The Ethics of International Trade"
to which I hope you will give
the honour of a perusal.
I am, Sir, Your obedient servant
Henri Lambert

St. Ermins Hotel,
St. James' Park, S.W.

18/11/16

Sir,

I take the liberty of sending you a pamphlet entitled « Un autre aspect de la question européenne une solution » with its English translation under the title « The Ethics of International Trade » <u>to</u> which I hope you will give the honour of a <u>perusal</u>.

I am, Sir, your obedient servant.

Henri Lambert

PARK AVENUE HOTEL
NEW YORK
FRED A. REED, PROPRIETOR
INC.

30th of Nov.ber 16

Dear Sir,

Dr David Starr Jordan
has had the kindness of sending
me the enclosed letter of introduction,
after having mentioned to you my
wish to have the honor of a
conversation with you.

I will be in New York

Friday, Saturday and Sunday
(and then away for probably a
fortnight) and any time at your
best convenience would suit me.

I take the liberty of sending
you enclosed a pamphlet on
"International Morality and Exchange".
The foot note of pages 22 & 23
will give you in two or three

David Starr Jordan
and
Jock [paw print] his mark.

David Starr Jordan (1851-1931).
President of Stanford University and leader of the
World Peace Foundation.

minutes a general idea of
my thesis.

I am

very sincerely yours
Henri Lambert

Park Avenue Hotel.
New York.

Col. E. M. House
115. East 53ᵈ St.
N. Y.

Park Avenue Hotel
New York

30th of Nov.ber 16

Dear Sir,

Dr David Starr Jordan has had the kindness of sending me the enclosed letter of introduction, after having mentioned to you my wish to have the honour of a conversation with you.

I will be in New York Friday, Saturday and Sunday (and then away for probably a fortnight) and any time at your best convenience would suit me.

I take the liberty of sending you enclosed a pamphlet on « International Morality and Exchange ». The foot note of pages 22 & 23 will give you in two or three minutes a general idea of my thesis.

I am very sincerely your's.

Henri Lambert

Park Avenue Hotel, New York

Col. E. M. House
115 East 53d S N.
N. Y.

II

Initial Contact -
Correspondence and Advice

Park Avenue Hotel
PARK AVENUE
(FOURTH AVENUE)
32ND & 33RD STREETS
FIRE PROOF

FRED. A. REED INC. PROPRIETOR.

New York
4th of December 16.

Dear Sir,

Allow me to express the opinion that the United States could not rightly join a "League of Nations" which would have as its object the enforcement on vanquished nations of an oppressive peace (as would "necessarily" be the peace dictated by the victors). It would neither be morally just nor be politically wise. Therefore the participation (forecasted) of the United States in such a League ought to be made conditional on the conclusion of a just peace.

Now, there can only be one just and only one durable peace — that by which and in which free or at least equal opportunities would be ~~offered by~~ afforded to and offered by all nations. For, economic needs being fundamental needs, economic liberty and justice are fundamental and primary liberty and justice

No international right or law is worthy of its name which does not provide for these necessities. Only ignorants or hypocrits can speak of an international law disregarding the fundamental and primary international liberty and justice for general economic opportunities. Unhappily there are many of such men in all European countries and in all sections or circles.

Humanity needs very much to be taught a great and high lesson. After such a lesson, a proposal coming from Germany (reduction of 50% of her customs duties, continuation of the Free Trade Policy by Great Britain; equality of opportunities in all colonies present and future) would be scorned and rejected the first month, discussed the second and considered favourably the third. The convocation of a peace conference would then have become fairly practicable and this conference would meet with some prospect of usefully discussing the numerous and difficult numerous European questions and of a successful result. For, there would not be an entire lack of the atmosphere of international good will and good faith, so indispensable for making peace and saving Europe!

Excuse me, dear Sir, and believe me, with great respect and regard, yours very sincerely   Henri Lambert

Park Avenue Hotel
32nd & 33rd Streets
New York

4th of December 16

Dear Sir,

Allow me to express the opinion that the United States could not rightly join a « League of Nations » which would have as its object the enforcement on vanquished nations of an oppressive peace (as would « <u>necessarily</u> » be the peace dictated by the victors). It would neither be morally just nor be politically wise. Therefore the participation (forecasted) of the United States in such a League ought to be made conditional on the conclusion of a just peace.

Now, there can only be <u>one</u> just and only <u>one</u> durable peace – that by which and in which free or at least equal opportunities would be afforded to and offered by all nations. For, economic needs being fundamental needs, economic liberty and justice are fundamental and primary liberty and justice.

No international right or law is worthy of its name which does not provide for these necessities. Only ignorants or hypocrites can speak of an international law disregarding the fundamental and primary international liberty and justice for general economic opportunities. Unhappily there are many of such men in <u>all</u> European countries and in <u>all</u> sections or wicles.

Humanity needs very much to be tought a great and high lesson. <u>After such a lesson</u>, a proposal coming from Germany (reduction of 50% of het customs duties ; continuation of the Free Trade Policy by Great Britain ; equality of opportunties in all colonies <u>present and future</u>) would be scorned and rejected the first month, discussed the second and considered favourably the third. The convocation of a peace conference would then have become fairly practicable and this conference would meet with some prospect of usefully discussing the numerous and difficult European questions and of a successful result. For, there would not be an entire lack of the atmosphere of international good will and good faith, so indispensable for making peace and saving Europe !

Excuse me, dear Sir, and believe me, with great respect and regard, your's very sincerely.

Henri Lambert

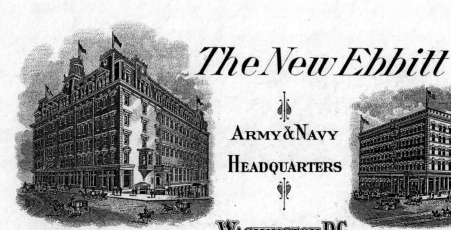

The New Ebbitt

ARMY & NAVY
HEADQUARTERS

WASHINGTON, D.C.

G. F. SCHUTT, Proprietor.
JAMES RUNCIMAN, Manager.

NATIONAL HOTEL
G. F. SCHUTT, Proprietor.

11ᵗʰ of December 1916.

Dear Sir,

Following the wish that you
have so kindly expressed, I give
instructions to the Bun Printing House,
New York, to send you as soon as
printed (probably to-morrow)
two copies of my pamphlet on
"The Economic Solution of the European

Crisis ". May I be allowed
to call your attention on the
" two letters on the European "problem"
Which follow the pamphlets as
an appendix ?

    I am, dear Sir,

        very sincerely yours

          Henri Lambert

P. S. My address will be the above
    for a fortnight.

Colonel House
115. E. 53° Street
   New York.

The New Ebbitt
Washington.D.G.

11th of December 1916

Dear Sir,

Following the wish that you have so kindly expressed, I give instructions to the Bun Printing House, New York, to send you as soon as printed (probably to-morrow) two copies of my pamphlet on « The Economic Solution of the European Crisis ». May I be allowed to call your attention on the « two letters on the European problem » which follow the pamphlet as an appendix ?

I am, dear Sir, very sincerely your's.

Henri Lambert

P.S. : My address will be the above for a fortnight.

Colonel House
115. E. 53^d Street
New York

The New Ebbitt Hotel in Washington.

III

Pursuance of Contacts -
Correspondence and Advice

Metropolitan Club
Washington, D.C.

20ᵗʰ of December 1916.

Dear Colonel House,

In my opinion, every thing tends to indicate that the German proposals will be broader than was first said, or supposed, and that they will have as their basis some practical measure of international increasing economic freedom. It is however unlikely that the case will be stated in an appealing way and that the basics will be shaped sufficiently broad for being acceptable without much improvement.

I have thought that it might interest you to have knowledge of this opinion, which is the result of a careful consideration of the great question „à l'ordre du jour".

I am, dear Colonel House, Very sincerely yours

Henri Lambert

Metropolitan Club
Washington, D. C.

20th of December 1916

Dear Colonel House,

In my opinion, every thing tends to indicate that the German proposals will be broader than was first said, or supposed, and that they will have as their basis some practical measure of international increasing economic freedom. It is however unlikely that the case will be stated in an appealing way and that the basics will be shaped sufficiently broad for being acceptable without much improvement.

I have thought that it might interest you to have knowledge of this opinion, which is the result of a careful consideration of the great question « à l'ordre du jour ».

I am, dear Colonel House, very sincerely your's.

Henri Lambert

Metropolitan Club
Washington, D.C.

Dear Colonel House,

My excuse for this new communication is in my good intentions.

If I interpret rightly what has happened, it has now become desirable that Germany gives her terms as soon as possible directly to Washington. I will suggest that it should be so, as I hope to have to-morrow the opportunity of doing so, discreetly and in the right quarters.

I am, dear Colonel House,
Very sincerely yours

Henri Lambert

22th of December 16.

Metropolitan Club
Washington, D. C.

22th of December 16

Dear Colonel House,

My excuse for this new communication is in my good intentions.

If I interpret rightly what has happened, it has now become desirable that Germany gives her terms as soon as possible directly to Washington. I will suggest that it should be so, as I hope to have tomorrow the opportunity of doing to, discreetly and in the right quarters.

I am, dear Colonel House, very sincerely your's,

Henri Lambert

PARK AVENUE HOTEL
NEW YORK

Friday evening

Dear Colonel House

I just end reading
President Wilson's speech and beg to
be allowed to respectfully express the
opinion that, of all the splendid
utterances of the President on the world
issues, this probably is the most magnificent
as well as the most important and

decisive. Its bearings upon the events of the near future and upon the destinies of mankind for all time cannot be estimated: they are incalculable.

With highest regards, I am, dear Colonel House, Very sincerely yours

Henri Lambert

Park Avenue Hotel
New York

Friday evening

Dear Colonel House,

I just ended reading President Wilson's speech and beg to be allowed to respectfully express the opinion that, of all the splendid attirances of the President on the world issues, this probably is the most magnificent as well as the most important and decisive. Its bearings upon the events of the war future and upon the destinies of mankind for all time cannot be estimated : they are incalculable.

With highest regards, I am, dear Colonel House very sincerely your's,

Henri Lambert

THE PARK AVENUE HOTEL, PARK AVENUE AND THIRTY FOURTH STREET.
From a photograph by R. F. Turnbull.

Park Avenue Hotel, New York.

Park Avenue Hotel

PARK AVENUE
(FOURTH AVENUE)
32 ND & 33 RD STREETS
FIRE PROOF

FRED. A. REED INC. PROPRIETOR.   JOHN R. MACDONALD. MGR.

New York

12ᵗʰ of January 17.

Dear Colonel House,

The Allies' reply to the President of
the United States offers to a great Statesman an
immense, unique, and perhaps even unhoped for,
opportunity for leading humanity in the ways of
the greatest conceivable progress towards international
liberty, justice, morality, peace and Civilization.

The responsibility for the War (not, obviously, for
the declaration of war, which is of secondary importance)
rests on all nations. The European War was bound
to come if the European nations persisted in their

policy of conquest, of establishment of selfish privileges, monopolies, of mutual exclusion (policy whe free-trade England supported in other nations and which she threatened to adopt for herself in the future)

If the great belligerent nations are really a. eager as they profess to be " to ensure the future respect of nationalities and the full security and liberty of their economic development, which all nations, great or small, (must) possess " there remain to the great nations no other way open than an agreement for future equality of economic opportunities offered by and afforded to all nations. For this is fundamental national necessity and fundamental international liberty, justice and morality. Without this, it would certainly " be impossible to attain a peace which would permit the establishment of the future of the European nations on a solid basis!"

Park Avenue Hotel
PARK AVENUE
(FOURTH AVENUE)
32ND & 33RD STREETS
FIRE PROOF

FRED. A. REED INC. PROPRIETOR.   JOHN R. MACDONALD. MGR.

New York

12½ of January 17.

II.

Moreover, the problems of Alsace-Lorraine, Poland, of Serbia, of the Bosporus, and of Belgium itself, as well as the colonial problem as a whole, — if considered in the interest and for the benefit of the occupants of those territories as well as of the whole World — can be solved definitely only in terms of "internationality", meaning political independance (for the first nationalities named) and extended economic rights, equality of opportunities in trade, insurance against future economic isolation and exclusion for all.

May I be finally allowed to state that in what concerns the " creation of a league of nations to ensure peace and justice throughout the world " the first requirement for a possible establishment and for the future successful <u>and peaceful</u> working of such a league, is that it should be based on economic liberty, justice and morality — which are fundamental liberty, justice and morality?

I am, dear Colonel House, with great respect and regard,

Very faithfully yours

Henri Lambert

Park Avenue Hotel
32nd & 33rd Streets
New York

12th of January 17

Dear Colonel House,

The Allies reply to the President of the United States offers to a great Statesman an immense, unique, and perhaps even unhoped for, opportunity for leading humanity in the ways of the greatest conceivable progress towards international liberty, justice, morality, peace and civilization.

The responsibility for the war (not, obviously, for the declaration of war, which is of secondary importance rest <u>on all nations</u>. The European war was bound to come if the European nations persisted in their policy of conquest, of establishment of selfish privileges, monopolies, of mutual exclusion (policy (un mot) free-trade England supported in other nations and which she threatened to adopt for herself in the future).

If the great belligerent nations are really as eager as they profess to be « to assure the future respect of nationalities and the full security and liberty of their economic development, which all nations, great or small, (must) possess » there remain to the great nations no other way open than an agreement for future equality of economic opportunity afforded to all nations. For this is a fundamental national necessity and fundamental international liberty, justice and morality. Without this, it would certainly « be impossible to attain a peace which would permit the establishment of the future of the European Nations on a solid basis ».

II

Moreover, the problems of Alsace-Lorraine, Poland, of Serbia, of the Bosforus, <u>and of Belgium itself</u>, as well as the colonial problem as a whole, – if considered in the interest and for the benefit of the occupants of those territories as well as of the whole world – can be solved <u>definitely</u> only in terms of « internationality », meaning political independence (for the first nationalities named) and extended economic rights, equality of opportunities in trade, insurance against future economic isolation and exclusion for all.

May I be finally allowed to state that in what concerns the « creation of a league of nations to ensure peace and justice throughout the world » the first requirement for a possible establishment and for the future successfull <u>and peaceful</u> working of such a league, is that it should be based on economic liberty, justice and morality – which are fundamental liberty, justice and morality ?

I am, dear Colonel House, with great respect and regard, very faithfully your's,

Henri Lambert

Park Avenue Hotel
PARK AVENUE
(FOURTH AVENUE)
32 ND & 33 RD STREETS
FIRE PROOF

FRED. A. REED INC. PROPRIETOR.　　　JOHN R. MACDONALD, MGR.

New York

14th of January 17.

Dear Colonel House,

No more powerful encouragement, no more decisive help could be given to Liberalism, Democracy and true Industrialism, not only in Europe but in the whole World — no more smashing and definitive blow could be struck on Reaction, Plutocracy, "Junkerism" in all countries, and on Militarism, — than would be such an attitude of the United States as would compel Germany to the resolution of seriously and immediately reducing her custom barriers. That formidable result can be obtained by the United States by a simple stroke of pen, without the least interference in the internal policy of the other nations: by intimating Europe that this great Republic cannot become a part in a League of Nations which would not proceed from, and be based on, the principle of Justice and Harmony and Peace involved in a future international policy of equality of economic opportunities in the whole World.

Immediately the Liberals and Democrats of England, Germany, Belgium and France, and of all neutral nations, would be inspirited, whilst ~~the~~ everywhere the depression of the reactionnairs would be awful. The English Jingoes and tariff-reformers, and all the other "economic-conferenciers of Paris" would feel that the ground has been irremediably cut under their feet. Of course, the British Government would answer that Great-Britain cannot pledge herself to Freetrade in a protectionist World (a great error, but very excusable). And Germany, as well as France, would be put in that so badly deserved situation; they would have immediately to choose between the adoption of a policy of freedom, justice and peace, or the acceptance of the responsibility for the continuation of this war and for the preservation of the whole unworthy regime which makes durable peace impossible and which makes even guarantees of it undesirable.

I often hear here people say that the high wages in the United States requires protectionism. The obvious truth is that the adoption by the U.S. of Freetrade (say, gradually, in 10 years) would increase the wages to 5, 10 or 15% and decrease the cost of life for at least 35%.

Believe me, dear Colonel House,
very sincerely yours
Henri Lambert

Park Avenue Hotel
32nd & 33rd Streets
New York

14th of January 17

Dear Colonel House,

No more powerful encouragement, no more decisive help could be given to Liberalism, Democracy and <u>true</u> Industrialism, not only in Europe but in the whole World – no more smashing and definitive blow could be struck on Reaction, Plutocracy, « Juncerisme » in <u>all</u> countries, and on Militarism, – than would be such an attitude of the United States as would compel Germany to the resolution of seriously, and immediately, reducing her custom barriers. That formidable result can be obtained by the United States by a simple stroke of pen, without the least interference in the internal policy of the other nations : by intimating to Europe that this great Republic cannot become a part in a League of Nations which would not proceed from, and be based on, the principle of Justice and Harmony and Peace invoiced in a future international policy of equality of economic opportunities in the whole world.

Immediately the Liberals and Democrats of England, Germany, Belgium and France, and of all neutral nations, would be inspirited whilst everywhere the depression of the reactionnaries would be awful. The English Jingoes and tariff-reformers, and all the other « economic-conferenciers of Paris « would feel that the ground has been irremediably cut under their feet. Of course, the British Government would answer that Great-Britain cannot pledge herself to Free Trade in a protectionist world (a great error, but very excusable). And Germany, as well as France, would be put in that so badly deserved situation : they would have immediately to choose between the adoption of a policy of freedom, justice and peace, or the acceptance of the responsibility for the continuation of this war and for the preservation of the whole unworthy regime which makes durable peace impossible and which makes even guarantees of it undesirable.

I often hear people say that the high wages in the United States requires protectionism. The obvious truth is that the adoption by the U. S. of Free Trade (say, gradually, in <u>10</u> years) would <u>increase</u> the wages to 5, 10 or 15% and decrease the cost of living by at least 35%.

Believe me, dear Colonel House, very sincerely your's,

Henri Lambert

Park Avenue Hotel
PARK AVENUE
(FOURTH AVENUE)
32 ND & 33 RD STREETS
FIRE PROOF

FRED. A. REED INC. PROPRIETOR.

New York
22ᵈ of January 17.

Dear Colonel House,

Men who are interested in my
propaganda (which keeps a private character) and who
approve my ideas have expressed some astonishment that I
never speak of the so injured and presently so distressed
interests of my countrymen and that I even never cite the
name of Belgium. I have answered them that Belgium
can be saved only by the Salvation of Europe. Whatever
intolerable may be the sufferings of the Belgian nation,
they must remain of a slight weight for the Statesmen
who are responsible for the fate of Great-Britain, France,
Russia, Italy, Germany and Austria. The man who
is intelligently devoted to the interests of Belgium must
be devoted first of all to the interests of Europe as a whole.

The European Statesmen are incapable of solving the European problem; it can only be solved from outside, because the belligerent Statesmen must deal with it from points of view which make the solution impossible. Even if they discussed it between themselves during ten years, it would not be, for that, nearer its solution.

The questions affecting the European problem, and facing the Statesmen of the whole world, are the following: Belgium, Alsace-Lorraine, Poland, Italia irredenta, the Balkan States, the Bosphorus, Asia-Minor, the German Colonies, the general colonial regime of the world, freedom of the seas, disarmament, international arbitration, League of Nations.

Not one of these problems can be escaped; and not one can be solved by an other way, by an other fundamental principle, by an other fundamental truth, than future international economic freedom, which is fundamental economic justice, morality, and security and Peace.

Only a peace having such a basis will be worth being maintained. Such a peace will not need being „enforced".

A thus established peace will maintain itself by general international consensus. And that will be the true League of Nations.

Accept, dear Colonel House, the expression of my great respect and regard

Henri Lambert

Park avenue Hotel
32nd & 33rd Streets
New York

22^d of January 17

Dear Colonel House,

Men who are interested in my propaganda (which keeps a private character) and who approve my ideas have expressed some astonishment that I never speak of the so injured and presently so distressed interests of my countrymen and that I even never cite the name of Belgium. I have answered them Belgium can be saved only by the salvation of Europe. Whatever intolerable may be the sufferings of the Belgian nation, they must remain of a slight weight for the Statesmen who are responsible for the fate of Great-Britain, France, Russia, Italy, Germany and Austria. The man who is intelligently devoted to the interests of Belgium must be devoted first of all to the interests of Europe <u>as a whole</u>.

The european Statesmen are incapable of solving the European problem ; it can only be saved from outside, because the belligerent Statesmen <u>must</u> deal with it from points of view which make the solution impossible. Even if they discussed it between themselves during ten years, it would not be, for that, nearer its solution.

The questions affecting the European problem, <u>and facing the Statesmen of the whole world</u>, are the following : Belgium, Alsace-Lorraine, Poland, Italia irredenta, the Balkan States, the Bosphorus, Asia-Minor, the German Colonies, the general colonial regime of the world, freedom of the seas, désarmament, international arbitration, League of Nations.

<u>Not one</u> of theses problems can be escaped ; and <u>not one</u> can be solved by an other way, by another fundamental principle, by another fundamental truth, than by future international economic freedom, which is fundamental economic justice, morality, security and Peace.

Only a peace having such a basis will be worth being maintained. Such a peace will not need being « enforced ». A thus established peace will maintain itself by general international consensus. And that will be the true League of Nations.

Accept, dear Colonel House, the expression of my respect and regard,

Henri Lambert

TELEGRAM.

The White House,

Washington.

14 WU JM 18   1055 am

PA., New York, Feb. 1,1917.

Col. E. M. House:

    Following my request in yesterday's letter I would much appreciate favor of conversation with you.

                       Henry Lambert,
                           Park Avenue Hotel.

– Letter 11 –

Telegram.

The White House,
Washington

14 WU JM 18
1055 am

PA., New York, Feb. 1, 1917.

Col. E. M. House :

Following my request in yesterday's letter I would much appreciate the favor of conversation with you.

Henry Lambert,

Park Avenue Hotel.

Park Avenue Hotel
PARK AVENUE
(FOURTH AVENUE)
32 ND & 33 RD STREETS
FIRE PROOF

FRED. A. REED INC. PROPRIETOR.

New York

2= of February 17.

Dear Colonel House,

I understand that I have no
regret to express that you prefer not to have
with me a conversation at present moment.

But, reading Tuesday evening and
Wednesday morning the extraordinary comments
on the German note of the whole press, of
all newspapers, I could not help being
frightened by the idea that there was a
general misunderstanding of this true meaning

of the note : « We are prepared to make peace on the basis of equality of economic rights; We are anxiously awaiting suggestions on that basis . »

– New reflections have convinced me that a misunderstanding is out of question .

Excuse me and believe me, dear Colonel House,

Yours very sincerely

Henri Lambert

Park Avenue Hotel
32nd & 33rd Streets
New York

2^{d} of February 17

Dear Colonel House,

I understand that I have no regret to express that you prefer not to have with me a conversation at present moment.

But reading Tuesday evening and Wednesday morning the extraordinary comments on the German note of the whole press, of <u>all</u> newspapers, I could not help being frightened by the idea that there was a <u>general</u> misunderstanding of this true meaning of the note : « We are prepared to make peace on the basis of equality of economic rights, we are anxiously awaiting suggestions on that <u>basis</u>. »

New reflections have convinced me that a misunderstanding is out of question.

Excuse me and believe me, dear Colonel House, your's very sincerely,

Henri Lambert

Park Avenue Hotel
PARK AVENUE
(FOURTH AVENUE)
32 ND & 33 RD STREETS
FIRE PROOF

FRED. A. REED INC. PROPRIETOR.

New York

5ᵗʰ of March 1917.

Dear Colonel House,

I have read with pleasure, joy and comfort the inaugural speech of the President. He is a splendid and powerful man and a skillful leader! I love him more and more and I trust in him.

The man who can save the World is living and he is where he should be.

Very sincerely yours

Henri Lambert

Park Avenue Hotel
32nd & 33rd Streets
New York

5th of March 1917

Dear Colonel House,

I have read with pleasure, joy and comfort the inaugural speech of the President. He is a splendid and powerful man and a skillful leader ! I love him more and more and I trust in him.

The man who can save the World is living and he is where he should be.

Very sincerely your's,

Henri Lambert

Colonel House.

Henri Lambert Esq.

   Park Avenue Hotel,   New York.

Dear Mr. Lambert:

        Just a line of thanks
for your kind words of appreciation of
the President which I shall send to
him to hearten him on his way.

        Sincerely yours,

115 East 53rd Street,   New York.

   March 8,   1917.

Henri Lambert Esq.
Park Avenue Hotel, New York.

Dear Mr. Lambert :

Just a line of thanks for your kind words of appreciation of the President which I shall send to him to hearten him on his way.

Sincerely your's,

House.

115 East 53rd Street, New York.

March 8, 1917.

Park Avenue Hotel
PARK AVENUE
(FOURTH AVENUE)
32 ND & 33 RD STREETS
FIRE PROOF

FRED. A. REED INC. PROPRIETOR.

New York 12th of March 17.

Dear Colonel House,

Not one moment had I thought that you would send my letter to President Wilson. I am the more glad that you did so, and happy, thinking that I may have, in some very humble measure, contributed to keep your ṿ dear President courageous and in good spirits.

I persist in my hopefulness. Surely the actual international law of neutrality is not founded on true international ethics. But the only thing to do is to apply it as it is, according to the letter of it. Surely also the whole international "law of war" entirely lacks true fundamental principles. But the Germans have to abide to the law which they have made, or accepted, and the only reasonable thing they can do is to trust the President of the United States for taking the right further step for peace. I am not without some confidence that v. Bernstorff will clear up the political atmosphere and the minds in Berlin, in respect to this.

I would like to be allowed, dear Colonel House, to draw your special attention on what appears to me to be a very important factor in the European problem — namely, that freedom of nationalities and freedom of the seas cannot intervene as causes of peace, — that they can only be consequences of it. Diverse important considerations make it impossible in practical policy, when dealing with the peace problem, to neglect or to be silent on these two very important questions. Nevertheless, they are not fundamental questions, they are not elements of the problem to be used for the "foundations" of the edifice of a reconstructed peaceful civilization. This edifice must, I think, be figured like this:

Individual political liberties.

National or collective liberties

International Security

Fundamental International Justice and Morality

Complete reform of the right of association and corporation (new right of co-operation) Profound reform of vote and Parliamentarism.

Freedom of nationalities; freedom of the seas and gradual disarmament on land and sea

Economic Security and Peace of Nations

Free Trade.
(Gradual reduction of customs duties in all countries and equality of economic rights in all colonies)

The liberties (national and individual) can be preserved only if resting on Security. This is what Sir Edward Grey in 1915 meant when he said that Great Britain was ready to discuss the question of "freedom of the seas" but that the condition making this freedom possible had first to be established. Fundamental security is economic security.

The liberals and democrats of the whole World will enthusiastically hail the man who will proclaim the fundamental international justice and morality. The number of those among the less progressive who, within some weeks, would join the movement, is enormous, unsuspected. I have on this subject made extraordinary experiences.

In the United States I have sometimes been objected that "free trade would mean free immigration". I have answered: Give an example of civilization; open the World to Humanity; give to "backward" peoples freer and better opportunities for making their living in their own country, by trading freely with them, and no excessive immigration shall be feared. All men prefer to live in their country provided they find there the possibilities of a decent economic and political life. Found civilization on natural realities and truths, and all the artificial causes of insecurity shall disappear; the international and national atmospheres will be healthy and the blossoms, flowers and fruits of Liberty will immediately appear, in all countries.

Excuse this letter, dear Colonel House, and believe me very faithfully yours Henri Lambert

Park Avenue Hotel
32nd & 33rd Streets
New York

12th of March 17

Dear Colonel House,

Not one moment had I thought that you would send my letter to President Wilson. I am the more glad that you did so, and happy, thinking that I may have, in some very humble measure, contributed to keep « our » dear President couragious and in good spirits.

I persist in my hopefulness. Surely the actual international law of neutrality is <u>not</u> founded on true international ethics. But the only thing to do is to apply it as it is, according to the letter of it. Surely also the whole international « law of war » entirely lacks true fundamental principles. But the Germans have to abide to the law which they have made, or accepted, and the only reasonable thing they can do is to trust the President of the United States for taking the right further step for peace. I am not without some confidence that V. Bernstorff will clear up the political atmosphere and the mind in Berlin, in respect to this.

I would like to be allowed, dear Colonel House, to draw your special attention on what appears to me to be a very important factor in the European problem – namely, that <u>freedom</u> of <u>nationalities</u> and <u>freedom of the seas</u> cannot intervene as <u>causes</u> of peace, – that they can only be <u>consequences</u> of it. Diverse important considerations make it impossible in practical policy, when dealing with the peace problem, to neglect or to be silent on these two very important questions. Nevertheless, they are not <u>fundamental</u> questions, they are not elements of the problem to be used for the « foundations » of the edifice of a reconstructed peaceful civilization.

This edifice must, I think, be figured like this :

Individual political liberties :
>   Complete reform of the right of association and
>   Corporation (newright of co-operation)
>   Profond reform of vote and parliamentarisme.

National or collective liberties :
>   Freedom of nationalities, Freedom of the seas
>   and Gradual disarmement on land and seas.

International Security :
>   Economic security and Peace of Nations.

Fundamental International
Justice and morality :
>   Free Trade.
>   (Gradual reduction of customs duties in all
>   Countries and equality of economic rights
>   in all colonies).

The liberties (national and individual) can be preserved only if resting on Security. This is what Sir Edward Grey in 1915 meant when he said that Great Britain was ready to discuss the question of « freedom of the seas » but that the condition making this freedom possible had first to be established. Fundamental security is economic security.

The liberals and democrats of the whole world will enthusiastically hail the men who will proclaim the fundamental international justice and morality. The number of those among the less progressive who, within some weeks, would join the movement, is enormous, unsuspected. I have on this subject made extraordinary experiences.

In the United States I have sometimes been objected that « freetrade would mean free immigration ». I have answered : give an example of civilization ; open the world to Humanity ; give to « backward » peoples freer and better opportunities for making their living in their own country, by trading freely with them, <u>and no excessive immigration shall be feared</u>. All men prefer to live in their country provided they find there the possibilities of a decent economic and political life. Found civilization on natural realities and truths, and all the artificial causes of insecurity shall disappear ; the international and national atmospheres will be healthy and the blossoms, flowers and fruits of Liberty will immediately appear, <u>in all countries</u>.

Excuse this letter, dear colonel House, and believe me very faithfully your's,

Henri Lambert

Park Avenue Hotel
PARK AVENUE
(FOURTH AVENUE)
32ND & 33RD STREETS
FIRE PROOF

FRED. A. REED INC. PROPRIETOR.

New York

19th of March 17.

Dear Colonel House,

I take the liberty of sending you a copy of *The Public* with an article on "Pax Romana and Pax Economica". It is not a "chef d'œuvre", but some useful thought is perhaps contained in it, so that the few minutes needed for reading it may not be a complete loss of time.

very faithfully yours

Henri Lambert

Park Avenue Hotel
32nd & 33rd Streets
New York

19th of March 17

Dear Colonel House,

I take the liberty of sending you a copy of <u>The Public</u> with an article on « Pax Romana and Pax Economica ». It is not a « chef d'œuvre » but some useful thought is perhaps contained in it, so that the few minutes needed for reading it may not be a complete loss of time.

Very faithfully your's,

Henri Lambert

Ajout d'un article de journal :

WANTS WILSON TO EXPLAIN.

Sonnino Seeks to Learn His Present Views on « Peace Without Victory. »

Special Cable to The New York Times.

ROME, March 17. – In a speech in the Chamber today Baron Sonnino, the Foreign Minister, discussed President Wilson's attitude toward the belligerents from Dec.18 when he wrote a note inspired « by high humanitarian sentiments and asked each group to indicate their peace conditions. » until the present Baron Sonnino wishes the President to explain how he proposes to obtain an international settlement guarateeing on humanity from the calamity of war and insuring the stability of small States if he adheres to his policy of seeking a « peace without victory.»

Park Avenue Hotel

PARK AVENUE
(FOURTH AVENUE)
32 ND & 33 RD STREETS
FIRE PROOF

FRED. A. REED INC. PROPRIETOR.

New York 3d of April 17.

Dear Colonel House,

Now that the President has spoken, I perhaps may allow myself, and be permitted by you, to express the conviction that the wise course has been chosen and the right thing done by him. For nearly three years he has done his utmost in order to keep his country out of war, to reestablish peace in the world, and so save civilization. He has succeeded in the first purpose so long as it has been a feasibility. He has not yet succeeded in the second great purpose, the restoration of peace in Europe, but for this he, in fact, is now in a position more favorable than was his before.

When, by laying the natural foundation of

of international good-will and harmony, this great, wise and courageous, leader of men will have removed the present peril, he will be able to successfully approach an other necessary and still greater undertaking — the laying of the natural foundation of democracy in the adequate, economic and political, liberty and <u>responsibility</u> of the individual — and he will save civilization from the equally grave, if less imminent, peril of irremediable social dissensions and of revolutions ending in anarchy.

Tragic as it is, yet the present time will appear as the most worthy for a strong man to have lived in.

Believe me, dear Colonel House, with great respect and regards,

Very faithfully yours

Henry Lambert

Park Avenue Hotel
32nd & 33rd Streets
New York

3^d of April 17

Dear Colonel House,

Now that the President has spoken, I perhaps may allow myself, and be permitted by you, to express the conviction that the wise course has been chosen and the right thing done by him. For nearly the years he has done his utmost in order to keep his country out of war, to reestablish peace in the world, and so save civilization. He has succeeded in the first purpose so long as it has been a feasibility. He has <u>not yet</u> succeeded in the second great purpose, in the second great purpose, the restoration of peace in Europe, but for this he, in fact, is now in a position more favorable than was his before.

When, by laying the natural foundation of international good will and harmony, this great, wise and courageous, leader of men will have removed the present peril, he will be able to successfully approach an other necessary and still greater undertaking – the laying of the natural foundation of democracy in the adequate, economic and political, liberty <u>and responsibility</u> of the individual – and he will save civilization from the equally grave, if less imminent, peril of irremediable social discusions and of revolutions ending in anarchy.

Tragic as it is, yet the present time will appear as the most worthy for a strong man to have lived in.

Believe me, dear Colonel House, with great respect and regards, very faithfully your's,

Henri Lambert

Park Avenue Hotel
PARK AVENUE
(FOURTH AVENUE)
32 ND & 33 RD STREETS
FIRE PROOF

FRED. A. REED IN C. PROPRIETOR.

New York
25 th of April 17

Dear Colonel House,

For a fortnight I have resisted my desire
to write you one more of these indiscrete letters, for which
the only possible excuse lies in the good intention which
dictates them — and in your kindness in reading them. But
I can no longer abstain from expressing the opinion that
in the true interests of Europe — and of future liberty,
peace and civilisation of in the whole World — it is to
be hoped for that this country will keep itself
diplomatically in as independent a position as possible,
that is to say, that, while giving its full military
help to the Allies, it will refuse to pledge itself
as to the ways, means and conditions of a peace settlement.

No doubt there is now and there will be for some days or weeks a very strong pressure toward such a pledge; but I am confident that the resistence will be adequate to the pressure... There appears to be in Europe, in any of the countries at war, no man capable of solving the international problem through means of force, nor any man capable of solving it through Truth — through liberty and Justice. The Europe and the World which would be shaped by the European Statesmen would be a hell and would unavoidably end in revolution and anarchy. M.ʳ Balfour knows what should be the solution, what is the only true solution (I know that he knows) but for expressing himself he is too cowardly (as are all highly intellectual but sceptical men, without convictions, incapable of enthusiasm for any thing — the exact psychology of M.ʳ Balfour) I moreover recognize that it will require courage for saying the Truth to the World.

The chances of saving Europe and civilization are, in my opinion, very slight. Europe cannot save herself; She must be saved against herself. The only hope is here. There is not the least doubt that the participation of this country in the war had become an unavoidable and a desirable thing in its own interest and in the interest of Mankind. But force cannot "solve" the problem and save the world, that is to say, end the war and make a peace compatible with disarmament and with social tranquillity and true amelioration.

Very faithfully yours

Henri Lambert

Park Avenue Hotel
32nd & 33rd Streets
New York

25th of April 17

Dear Colonel House,

For a fortnight I have resisted my desire to write you one more of these indiscrete letters for which the only possible excuse lies in the good intention which dictates them – and in your kindness in reading them. But I can no longer abstain from expressing the opinion that in the <u>true</u> interests of Europe – and of future liberty, peace and civilization in the whole world – it is to be hoped for that this country will keep itself <u>diplomatically</u> in as independent a position as possible, that is to day, that, while giving full military help to the allies, it will refuse to pledge itself as to the ways, means and conditions of a peace settlement. No doubt there is now and there will be for some days or weeks a very strong pressure toward such a pledge ; but I am confident that the resistance will be adequate to the pressure…

There appears to be in Europe, or in any of the countries at war, no man capable of solving the international problem through means of force, nor any man capable of solving it through Truth – through liberty and justice. The Europe and the World which would be shaped by the European statesmen would be a hell and would unavoidably end in revolution and anarchy. Mr Balfour <u>knows</u> what should be the solution, what <u>is</u> the only true solution (I know that he knows) but for expressing himself he is too cowardly (as are all hightly intellectual but sceptical men, without convictions, incapable of enthusiasm for anything – the exact psychology of Mr Balfour) I moreover recognize that it will require courage for saying the Truth to the world.

The chances of saving Europe and civilization are, in my opinion, very slight. <u>Europe cannot save herself</u>; she must be saved <u>against</u> herself. The only hope is <u>here</u>. There is not the least doubt that the participation of this country in the war had become an unavoidable and a desirable thing in its own interest and in the interest of mankind. But force cannot « solve » the problem and save the world, that is to say, end the war and make a peace compatible with disarmament and with social tranquillity and true amelioration.

Very faithfully your's,

Henri Lambert

Park Avenue Hotel
PARK AVENUE
(FOURTH AVENUE)
32 ND & 33 RD STREETS
FIRE PROOF

FRED. A. REED INC. PROPRIETOR.

New York
13th of May 17.

Dear Colonel House,

I have received from Holland the enclosed paper, which I take the liberty of sending you in the thought that a passage of it (which I have marked) may interest you.

Before going back to Europe — probably next month — I would very much appreciate the favor of a conversation with you.

I am, dear Colonel House,
very sincerely yours

Henri Lambert

Park Avenue Hotel
32nd & 33rd Streets
New York

13th of May 17

Dear Colonel House,

I have received from Holland the enclosed paper, which I take the liberty of sending you in the thought that a passage of it (which I have marked) may interest you.

Before going back to Europe – probably next month – I would very much appreciate the favor of a conversation with you.

I am, dear Colonel House, very sincerely your's,

Henri Lambert

Residence of Edward M. House in Austin (Texas).

Henri Lambert Esq.

Park Avenue Hotel, New York.

Dear Mr. Lambert:

Will you not ring my secretary up over telephone Plaza 6061 on Friday of this week so that an engagement may be made for us to meet that day.

Sincerely yours,

115 East 53rd Street, New York.

May 14, 1917.

Henri Lambert Esq.

Park Avenue Hotel
New York

Dear Mr Lambert :

Will you not ring my secretary up over telephone Plaza 6061 on Friday of this week so that an engagement may be made for us to meet that day.

Sincerely your's,

115 East 53rd Street, New York.

May 14, 1917.

Park Avenue Hotel
PARK AVENUE
(FOURTH AVENUE)
32 ND & 33 RD STREETS
FIRE PROOF

FRED. A. REED INC. PROPRIETOR.   JOHN R. MACDONALD MANAGER.

New York
4th of June 17.

Dear Colonel House,

I need not say that day and night I think over the situation of Europe, of my country and of this country. No doubt many others in the world do the same thinking, but I cannot help fearing that there be but a very few who concentrate their thought more objectively and impartially on the general causes and issues involved in the international question.

The difficulty and even the danger of persisting at present in peace making efforts are undeniable. Much can be said against any such step. But the diverse perils arising from an abandonment of the ways of peace through truth and justice are <u>immensely</u> greater.

The situation of the world is more than serious. But it is not desperate, provided the spirit of Democracy can be stirred up in our Countries and in the <u>Central Empires</u>. This can only be done by proposing to the peoples of all countries an ideal of freedom and justice. Enthusiasm shall more and more vanish for schemes of conquest and even of remodeling of nations. Workmen and peasants, more than great businessmen and politicians, are accessible to ideals, when these are clear, simple and true. An ideal of future peace made secure by liberty and justice in the international relations concerned with the "making of a living", would appeal – and rightly appeal – to the

The Russian, the English, the American, the German, the Austrian workman and peasants do not desire to deprive the other workmen of the opportunity of making their living. They are able to understand what an injustice, a monstrosity, a crime that is.

A proposal of universal <ins>peace through</ins> economic freedom, equality and justice would stir up the enthusiasm not only of the workmen and peasants but also of the liberal and democratic opinion <u>in all nations</u>. It would <u>immediately</u> find a response and strong support in all neutral countries without a single exception. It would very favorably be looked upon by all German elements in the neutral countries and here. Within two months the German and Austrian rulers would be obliged to speak plainly; they would be compelled to deal with the questions from a new angle. If they refused to take the new point of view, the fight between the liberals and democrats and the autocrats would <u>really begin</u> in Germany and Austria.

"<u>Gradual disarmament</u> and permanent peace through economic justice" should be the "motto". Of course, such a proposal would immediately be called "mischievous" in certain quarters in all belligerent nations; but before one week of public discussion the international skies would appear to have been extraordinarily cleared up. It is inconceivable to me, dear Colonel House, that millions and millions of young men and innocent people shall die, that civilization shall perish, <u>the only possible solving word</u> having remained to be said.

With high regards and respects very faithfully yours Henri Lambert

4th of June 17.

Whatever may be in the belligerent countries the diverse opinions on the necessary result of the international conflict, there seems to exist everywhere a unanimity of opinion on this: the future world must be a world of security and peace.

Surely there are very different conceptions as to the ways and means of attaining such a result.

In the enemy countries there appears to be a majority of men, even among the leaders, who, inspired by a monstrous national egotism, conceive security and peace possible only in the submission of other nations,- if not of the whole world,-to the selfish will and interests of would be conquerors and dominators. But history shows that empire after empire, civilization after civilization, has broken down on account of that conception and less than ever before could such a scheme be carried through. The world never more shall know a peace resembling the Pax Romana" — or a peace much worse than this was.

In our democratic countries, the vast majority of citizens think that security and peace can be established and preserved only through liberty and justice. We also want the nations to submit to a will and to an interest — but these are the will of common liberty and the interest of common justice. For these ideals every one among us is gladly prepared to give his wealth, his life, the life of his dearest ones.

Nor do we lose sight of the fundamental necessity of a peace based on freedom and justice — of the necessary realities of any durable peace.

Every freedom and justice loving man feels and knows that he has the right of claiming for himself and the duty of claiming for others the opportunity of „making his living". No social security and peace within a community are conceivable if the citizens hamper that right and fail in that duty.

The necessity of economic justice and security is even more imperative if the relations between nations are considered. No international peace can conceivably be founded and maintained, unless nations accord to each other equality of rights and opportunities for „making their living" and developing peacefully. A peace durable and just, — durable because just — the only possible durable peace — must be based on equality of international economic opportunities and on complete reciprocity in trade agreements. Durable peace must be a „Pax Economica," to be summed up in these few words: gradual disarmament on land and sea, with free, equal and reciprocal economic rights for all nations, great and small.

Once this fundamental principle is agreed upon, all other necessary agreements — such as territorial readjustments, indemnities to sacrificed peoples, internal reforms — should become possible and even easy.

Park Avenue Hotel
32nd & 33rd Streets
New York

4th of June 17

Dear Colonel House,

I need not say that day and night I think over the situation of Europe, of my country and of this country. No doubt many others in the world do the same thinking, but I cannot help fearing that there be but a very few who concentrate their thought more objectively and impartially on the general causes and issues involved in the international question.

The difficulty and even the danger of persisting at present in peace making efforts are undeniable. Such can be said against any such step. But the diverse perils arising from an abandonment of the ways of peace through truth and justice are <u>immensely</u> greater.

The situation of the world is more than serious. But it is not desperate, provided the spirit of Democracy can be stirred up in our countries <u>and in the Central Empires</u>. This can only be done by proposing to the peoples of all countries an ideal of freedom and justice. Enthusiam shall more and more vanish for schemes of conquest and even of remodeling of nations. Workmen and peasants, more than great businessmen and politicians, are accessible to ideals, when these are <u>clear</u>, <u>simple</u> and <u>true</u>. An ideal of future peace made secure by liberty and justice in the international relations <u>concerned with the « making of a living »</u>, would appeal – and rightly appeal – to them. The Russian, the English, the American, the German, the Austrian workmen and peasants do not desire to deprive te other workmen of the opportunity of making their living. They are able to understand what an injustice, a monstruosity, a crime that is.

A proposal of universal peace through economic freedom, equality and justice would stir up the enthusiasm not only of the workmen and peasants but also of the liberal and democratic opinion <u>in all nations</u>. It would <u>immediately</u> find a response and strong support in all neutral countries without a single exception. It would very favorably be looked upon by all German elements in the neutral countries and here. Within two months the German and Austrian rulers would be obliged to speak plainly ; they would be compelled to deal with the questions from a new angle. If they refused to take the new point of view, the fight between the liberals and democrats and the autocrats would <u>really begin</u> in Germany and Austria.

« <u>Gradual disarmament and permanent peace through economic justice</u> » should be the motto. Of course, such a proposal would immediatly be called « mischievous » in certain quarters in all belligerent nations ; but before one week of public discussion the international skies would appear to have been extraordinarily cleared up.

It is inconceivable to me, dear Colonel House, that millions and millions of young men and innocent people shall die, that civilisation shall perish, <u>the only possible solving word</u> having remained to be said.

With high regards and respest very faithfully your's,

Henri Lambert

4th of June 17

Whatever may be in the belligerent countries the diverse opinions on the necessary result of the international conflict, there seems to exist everywhere a unanimity of opinion on this : the future world must be a world of security and peace. Surely there are very different conceptions as to the ways and means of attaining such result.

In the enemy countries the appears to be a majority of men, even among the leaders, who, inspired by a monstrous national egotism, conceive security and peace possible only in the submission of other nations, – if not of the whole world – to the selfish will and interests of would be conquerors and dominators. But history shows that empire after empire, civilization after civilization, has broken down on account of that conception and less than ever before could such a scheme be carried through the world-never more shall it know a peace resembling the « Pax Romana » - a peace much worse than this was.

In our democratic countries, the vast majority of citizens think that security and peace can be established and preserved only through liberty and justice. We also want the nations to submit to a will and to an interest – but these are the will of common liberty and the interest of common justice. For these ideals every one among us is gladly prepared to give his wealth, his life, the life of his dearest ones.

Nor do we lose sight of the fundamental necessity of a peace based on freedom and justice – of the necessary realities of any durable peace.

Every freedom and justice loving man feels and knows that he has the right of claiming for himself and the duty of claiming for others the opportunity of « making his living ». No social security and peace within a community are conceivable if the citizens hamper that right and fail in that duty.

The necessity of economic justice and security is even more imperative if the relations between nations are considered. No international peace can conceivably be founded and maintained, unless nations accord to each other equality of rights and opportunities for « making their living » and developing peacefully. A peace durable and just – durable because just – the only possible durable peace – must be based on equality of international economic opportunities <u>and on complete reciprocity in trade agreements</u>. Durable peace must be a « Pax Economica », to be summed up in these few words : <u>gradual disarmement on land and sea, with free, equal and reciprocal economic rights for all nations, great and small</u>.

Once this fundamental principle is agreed upon, all other necessary agreements – such as territorial readjustments, indemnities to sacrificed peoples, internal reforms – should become possible and even easy.

Park Avenue Hotel
PARK AVENUE
(FOURTH AVENUE)
32 ND & 33 RD STREETS
FIRE PROOF
PARK, INC.

FRED A. REED, INC., PROPRIETOR.
GEO. C. BROWN, PRESIDENT

JOHN R. MACDONALD MANAGER.
W. P. MERRITT, ASS'T MGR.

New York
10 th of July 1917.

Dear Colonel House,

I take the liberty of sending you enclosed two copies of a „ Message to the Society of Friends „.

I am, dear Colonel House, with high regard

Very sincerely yours

Henri Lambert

P.S. I have delayed my departure to Europe, my son being called to the Belgian army for beginning of next year only.

Colonel E. M. House
115. E. 53 Street
New York.

Park Avenue Hotel
32nd & 33rd Streets
New York

10th of July 1917

Dear Colonel House,

I take the liberty of sending you enclosed two copies of a « message to the Society of Friends. »

I am, dear Colonel House, with high regard, very sincerely your's,

Henri Lambert

P.S. I have delayed my departure to Europe, my son being called to the Belgian army for beginning of next year only.

Colonel E. M. House
115 E 53^d Street
New York

Park Avenue Hotel
PARK AVENUE
(FOURTH AVENUE)
32 ND & 33 RD STREETS
FIRE PROOF
PARK, INC.

FRED A. REED INC.

GEO. C. BROWN, PRESIDENT

JOHN R. MACDONALD, MANAGER.

W. P. MERRITT, ASS'T MGR.

New York 19-VII 17.

Dear Colonel House,

I read with great satisfaction in the papers this evening that the United States have refused to attend the Paris Conference on the Balkan question. The more carefully the United States shall abstain from intervening in the ignoble diplomacy of Europe (while lending its full military and financial support to the Allies) the better it will be for this country and for Europe. The opportunity of rendering to Europe against Europe immense diplomatic services is coming, maybe very rapidly.

I suppose I do not need calling your attention on the recent declaration of the „majority bloc" of the Reichstag: "only an economic peace can prepare the ground for a friendly association of the nations. It is probably the first announcement of a great victory for our ideas.

But how sorry I am that the proposal of an "economic peace" did not come from here. I think that I would accept to see the war lasting one month more rather than to see the „economic peace" proposed by Germany. Moreover it perhaps is more easy to propose than to support. Very faithfully yours Henri Lambert

Park Avenue Hotel
32nd & 33rd Streets
New York

19/VII/17

Dear Colonel House,

I read with great satisfaction in the papers this evening that the United States have refused to attend the Paris conference on the Balkan question. The more carefully the United States shall abstain from intervening in the ignoble diplomacy of Europe (while lending its full military and financial support to the allies) the better it will be for this country <u>and for Europe</u>. The opportunity of rendering <u>to Europe against Europe</u> immense diplomatic services is coming, maybe very rapidly.

I suppose I do not need calling your attention on the recent declaration of the « majority bloc » of the Reichstag : « <u>only an economic peace can prepare the ground for a friendly association of the nations</u> ». It is probably the first announcement of a great victory for our ideas.

But how sorry I am that the proposal of an « economic peace » did not come from here. I think that I would accept to see the war lasting one month more rather than to see the « economic peace » proposed by Germany. Moreover it perhaps is more easy to propose than to support.

Very faithfully your's,

Henri Lambert

Park Avenue Hotel
PARK AVENUE
(FOURTH AVENUE)
32ND & 33RD STREETS
FIRE PROOF

~~FRED A. REED~~ Inc.
GEO. C. BROWN, PRESIDENT

JOHN R. MACDONALD, MANAGER.
W. P. MERRITT, ASS'T MANAGER

New York

Dear Colonel House,

I take the liberty of sending you the editorial page of the _Springfield Republican_ of yesterday with an article which, I have thought, may interest you.

More and more it appears that the only possible conclusive settlement is an "economic peace".

With high regards, I am,
Dear Colonel House,
Very faithfully yours
Henri Lambert

15th of August 17.

– Letter 24 –

Park Avenue Hotel
32nd & 33rd Streets
New York

15th of August 17

Dear Colonel House,

I take the liberty of sending you the editorial page of the <u>Spring field Republican</u> of yesterday with an article which, I have thought, may interest you.

More and more it appears that the only possible conclusive settlement is an « economic peace. »

With high regards, I am, dear Colonel House, very faithfully your's,

Henri Lambert

Park Avenue Hotel
PARK AVENUE
(FOURTH AVENUE)
32 ND & 33 RD STREETS
FIRE PROOF

FRED. A. REED Inc. ~~PROPRIETORS~~
GEO. C. BROWN, PRESIDENT

JOHN R. MACDONALD MANAGER.
W. P. MERRITT, ASS'T MANAGER

New York 29th of August 17

Dear Colonel House,

I take the liberty of sending you two copies of a booklet entitled "Pax Economica," of which, I think, Parts III and IV may interest you. Parts I & II are a reprint of my former pamphlets, which you have done me the honor to read.

It has been with keen interest and very great satisfaction that I have read the reply of the President to the

peace message of the Pope. It is a
splendid, a masterful statement and
within a short time, it will have an
immense influence on the ideas and the
attitude of the liberal and democratic elements
in the whole World and, more than anywhere
else, in Germany and in Austria. My joy
is great that the real impulse to the
economic peace will have come from a
Republic. For, I am a Republican; my
father, who was during more than 30 years a
Member of the Belgian Parliament, was one of
the two or three known Belgian Republicans (he
had come several times to America and knew
Mr Lincoln) and he made me a Republican before
I was twelve years old. To my delight this
morning, after being read the Statement of the
President, I have taken the liberty of sending him a
telegram of congratulation.   Very sincerely yours

Henri Lambert

Park Avenue Hotel
32nd & 33rd Streets
New York

29th of August 17

Dear Colonel House,

I take the liberty of sending you two copies of a booklet entitled « Pax Economica, » of which, I think, Parts III and IV may interest you. Parts I & II are a reprint of my former pamphlets, which you have done me the honor to read.

It has been with keen interest and very great satisfaction that I have read the reply of the President to the peace message of the Pope. It is a splendid, a masterful statement and within a short time, it will have an immense influence on the ideas and the attitude of the liberal and democratic elements in the whole world and, <u>more than anywhere else</u>, in Germany and in Austria. My joy is great that the real impulse to the <u>economic peace</u> will have come from a Republic. For, I am a Republican ; my father, who was during more than 30 years a member of the Belgian Parliament, was one of the two or three known Belgian Republicans (he has come several times to America and knew Mr Lincoln) and he made me a Republican before I was twelve years old. In my delight this morning, after having read the statement of the President, I have taken the liberty of sending him a telegram of congratulation.

Very sincerely your's,

Henri Lambert

Famous Sunken Palm Garden, as seen from the Dining Verandas, Park Avenue Hotel.

M. Henri Lambert,

      Hotel Vanderbilt, New York.

Dear M. Lambert:

      I knew you would like the
President's reply to the Pope for it points
in the direction of your own views.

      I shall be in New York at the end
of September and it will be a pleasure to
see you again.

      Sincerely yours,

Magnolia, Massachusetts.

    August 31, 1917.

Colonel House (1858-1938).

IV

Major Advice on negotiation of a Peace Treaty and Armistice

Park Avenue Hotel
PARK AVENUE
(FOURTH AVENUE)
32 ND & 33 RD STREETS
FIRE PROOF

FRED. A. REED INC. PROPRIETOR.   JOHN R. MACDONALD MANAGER.

New York 24th of Sept 17.

Dear Colonel House,

I would in the present circumstances like to be permitted to express these opinions:

1) the deep, wholesome and necessary branding of "Kaiserism" by President Wilson's reply to the Pope being a thing done and well done, we should now help the healing of the wound, or at least avoid irritating it, and let it become a scar — indeed a permanent scar.

The peace-wishes expressed by Germany are sincere, though the satisfaction given to the demands of the President of the United States are not — not yet — sufficient. They are in preparation; it is a question of two or three weeks. The Reichstag will express, with full approval of the Government, also that Germany is prepared to evacuate France and to restore Belgium provided she ~~Germany~~ is ensured ~~assured~~ of future free economic opportunities. This will be only the beginning and announcement of economic offers.

The ~~perts~~ of the note of Germany to the Pope which is

an indirect reply to President Wilson is, in fact, honorable.

The President of the United States is the master of the world's situation. Happily for us, he will be „a good master".

2) the Russian situation is very nearly hopeless. Kerensky may be the only possible man in Russia, but he is a sentimental much more than an intellectual idealist and can therefore only be a second or third rate statesmen — where a superhuman statesman is needed. That the Russian nation was going to be in anarchy for several years was very nearly a certainty from the first day of the revolution. Nothing must be expected from there.

3) the French situation is not good; it might become bad (though never so bad as the Russian) if the war were to last one year more. I have lived during the last ten years before the war the greatest part of the time in Paris and France and I think that I pretty well understand the soul of the French people and interpret the symptoms of the French politics.

An important thing, never to lose sight of, is that within a maximum of three years after reestablishment of peace, the social situation in France, Italy, Belgium and England will become very acute, maybe extremely grave. This is an absolute certainty. The only prospect and hope of seeing a similar situation develop in Germany is through a peace without injustice and oppression — a „peace without victory". If the peace concluded were oppressive and spoliative, an extraordinary opportunity for a war of revenge and liberation would be afforded to the Germans before 10 years.

But this is another question. I will take the liberty of writing you, dear Colonel House, in a few days on the social problem, on which I hold views which are entirely original and, I think, of real interest.

Excuse this too long letter and believe me very sincerely yours Henri Lambert

Park Avenue Hotel
32nd & 33rd Streets
New York

24th of september 17

Dear Colonel House,

I would in the present circumstances like to be permitted to express these opinions :

1. The deep, wholesome and necessary branding of « Kaiserisme » by President Wilson's reply
to the Pope being a thing done and well done, we should now help the healing of the wound, or at least avoid irritating it, and let it become a scar – indeed a permanent scar.

The peace-wishes expressed by Germany are sincere, though the satisfaction given to the demands of the President of the United States are not – <u>not yet</u> – sufficient. They are in preparation ; it is a question of two or three weeks. The Reichstag will express, with full approval of the government, also that Germany is prepared to evacuate France and to restore Belgium provided she is ensured of future free economic opportunities. This will be only the beginning and announcent of economic offers.

The part of the note of Germany to the Pope which is an indirect reply to President Wilson is, in fact, <u>humble</u>. The President of the United States <u>is</u> the master of the world's situation.Happily for us, he will be « a good master ».

2. The Russian situation is very nearly hopeless. Kercensky may be the only possible man in Russia, but he is a sentimental much more than an intellectual idealist and can therefore only be a second or third rate statesman – where a superhuman statesman is needed ? That the Russian nation was going to be in anarchy for several years was very nearly a certainty from the first day of the revolution. Nothing must be expected from there.

3. The French situation is <u>not good</u> ; it might become had (though never so bad as the Russian) if the war were to last one year more. I have lived during the last ten years before the war the greatest part of the time in Paris and France and I think that I pretty well understand the soul of the French people and interpret the symptoms of the French politics.

An important thing, never to lose sight of, is that within a maximum of three years after restablishment of peace, the social situation in France, Italy, Belgium and England will become very acute, maybe extremely grave. <u>This is an absolute certainty</u>. The only prospect and hope of seing a similar situation develop in Germany is through a peace without injustice and oppression – a « peace without victory ». If the peace concluded were oppressive and spoliative, an extraordinary opportunity, for a war of revenge <u>and liberation</u> would be afforded to the Germany before 10 years.

But this is another question. I will take the liberty of writing you, dear Colonel House, in a few days on the social problem, on which I hold views which are entirely original and, I think, of real interest. Excuse this too long letter and believe me very very sincerely your's,

Henri Lambert

Park Avenue Hotel
PARK AVENUE
(FOURTH AVENUE)
32 ND & 33 RD STREETS
FIRE PROOF

FRED. A. REED INC. PROPRIETOR.   JOHN R. MACDONALD MANAGER.

New York 26th of Sept
17.

Dear Colonel House,

What I expected from a near future has happened sooner than foreseen. According to the papers of this evening, Germany offers the restoration of Belgian independence (and consequently the evacuation of France) provided "economic concessions" are made to her. The desired guarantees concern chiefly Antwerp, where Germany has big and *natural* interests, — this port being by nature of things the way out and the outlet of a very important part of Germany. The guarantees desired may therefore not be illegitimately desired.

The method of dealing with this question is not by simply and purely answering that no guaranties of any kind are to be given to Germany. Of course, this answer being stupid has a great chance of being made. But the true, wise attitude would be to say to the Germans: "You ask for economic concessions. Which are *yours*?" And probably it is such a query, that Germany expects, awaits, and is ready to answer to.

An other German "condition" of the restoration of Belgium is that there be in future an "administrative division" between the Flemish and Walloon populations. This is desired by many Flemish and by a not negligible minority of Walloons. Of course, the Germans must not be allowed to try to pose as the benefactors of a part of the Belgian people. But in itself the suggestion is by no means unreasonable. The truth is that the "oppressed" are not the Flemish, but the Walloons; I always have refused to take publicly an interest in this ~~silly~~ question but I have a very definite opinion on it : if absolute international security were established in Europe under the régime of an economic peace, the "administrative separation" of the two Belgian elements of population "would be an excellent and happy thing for both. Provided, of course, the two administratively separated parts were ~~for~~ economically federated under a system of absolute free-trade.

This question must be approached indirectly, from – if I may say, – from a "lateral side"; for, the real reason of the political "sollicitude" of Germany for the Flemish is economic. This, as far as I can see, is understood by nobody, though it is very simple. The Germans hope to get along pretty well with the ~~Germans~~ Flemish in the future, but not with the Walloons; Antwerp is a Flemish place; the Germans would like to develop Antwerp, as a port, and their means of communications between the Rhine and Antwerp;

Park Avenue Hotel

PARK AVENUE
(FOURTH AVENUE)
32 ND & 33 RD STREETS
FIRE PROOF

FRED. A. REED IN C. PROPRIETOR.   JOHN R. MACDONALD MANAGER.

New York

II

if there were an "administrative separation," they could hope to indirectly have the economic control or leadership of the Flemish country. But this would be a great international danger. Therefore, the right answer, — that which would not go against natural necessities, — would be this : the question of the future administrative separation concerns us Belgians, and not you Germans ; we understand your views and plans ; what you really want is economic facilities and guarantees for the future. But, once more, what are your economic concessions to the whole of Belgium — to be followed or accompanied by same concessions, made to all your present enemies ?

As a past, present, and future guarantor

of Belgium's independence, the United States want to have, or must have, an exact view of this important point. <u>And this is the only exact view</u>.

Believe me, dear Colonel House,
Very sincerely yours
Hari Lambert

P. S. When I say that we ought to avoid irritating the wound caused on "Kaiserism" by the branding note of the President, I have not ~~especially~~ in mind the disclosure of the Luxburg and Bernstorff affairs but much more the declarations by "high officials" that no peace shall be made with the Germans unless they have first got rid of the Hohenzollern dynasty. This will come, but surely not during the war.

Park Avenue Hotel
32nd & 33rd Streets
New York

26th of September 17

Dear Colonel House,

What I expected from a near future has happened sooner than foreseen. According to the papers of this evening, Germany offers the restoration of Belgian independence (and consequently the evacuation of France) provided « economic concessions » are made to her. The desired guarantees concern chiefly Antwerp, where Germany has big <u>and natural</u> interest, – this post being by nature of things the way out and the outlet of a very important part of Germany. The guarantees <u>may</u> therefore not be illegitimitely desired.

The method of dealing with this question is not by simply and purely answering that no guaranties of any kind are to be given to Germany. Of course, this answer being stupid has a great chance of being made. But the true, wise attitude would be to say to the Germans : « You ask for economic concessions. Which are <u>yours ?</u> » and probably it is such a query, that Germany expects, awaits and is ready to answer to.

Another German « condition » of the restoration of Belgium is that there be in future an « administrative division « between the Flemish and Walloon populations. This is desired by many Flemish and by a not negligible minority of Walloons. Of course, the Germans must not be allowed to try to pose as the benefactors of a part of the Belgian people. But in itself the suggestion is by no means unreasonable. The truth is that the « oppressed » are not the Flemish, but the Walloons ; I always have refused to take publicly an interest in this question but I have a very definite opinions on it : <u>if absolute international security were established in Europe under the regime of an economic peace</u>, the « administrative separation » of the two Belgian elements of population would be an excellent and happy thing <u>for both</u>. Provided, <u>of course</u>, the two administratively separated parts were economically federated under a system of absolute free-trade.

This question must be approached indirectly, from, – if I may say so – from a « literal side » ; for the real reason of the political « solicitude » of Germany for the Flemish is economic. This, as far as I can see, is understood by nobody, though it is very simple. The Germans hope to get along pretty well with the Flemish in the future, but not with the Walloons ; Antwerp is a Flemish place ; the Germans would like to develop Antwerp, as a port, and as their means of communications between the Rhine and Antwerp ;

II

If there were an « administrative separation « they could hope to indirectly have the economic control or leadership of the Flemish country. But this would be a great international danger. Therefore, the right answer, – <u>that which would not go against natural necessities</u>, – would be this : the question of the future administrative separation concerns <u>us</u> Belgians, and <u>not</u> <u>you</u> Germans ; we understand your views and places ; what you <u>really</u> want is <u>economic facilities and guarantees for the future</u>. But, once more, what are <u>your</u> economic concessions <u>to the whole of Belgium</u> – to be followed or accompanied by same concessions, made to all your present ennemies ?

As a past, present, and future guarantor of Belgium's independence, the United States want to have, or must have, an exact view of this important point. <u>And this is the only exact view</u>.

Believe me, dear Colonel House, very sincerely your's,

Henri Lambert

P.S. When I say that me ought to avoid irritating the wound caused on « Kaiserism » by the branding note of the President, I have not in mind the disclosure of the Luxburg and Bernstorff affairs but much more the declarations by « high officials » that no peace shall be made with the Germans unless they have first got rid of the Hohenzollern dynasty. This will come, but surely not during the war.

Park Avenue Hotel
PARK AVENUE
(FOURTH AVENUE)
32ND & 33RD STREETS
FIRE PROOF

FRED A. REED, INC. PROPRIETOR.
GEO. C. BROWN, PRESIDENT.

JOHN R. MACDONALD, MANAGER.
W. P. MERRITT, ASS'T MANAGER.

New York 1th of October 17

Dear Colonel House,

I have been asking myself which should and could be the guarantees requisite from Germany and her Government for the stability and durability of the future treaty of peace.

The „ousting" of the Hohenzollern dynasty seems to me, and probably to some others, to be an „excessive" demand. The adoption of a Government responsible to the Parliament is not an easy measure to be carried through; moreover it would not be a very serious guarantee (in my opinion it is even very questionable whether such a government is a real progress in the Parliamentary system)

I suggest that the necessary guarantee

should be this : Germany should have at

the peace conference one half of her delegates
designated
~~delegated~~ directly by the Reichstag ; these delegates,

as well as those designated by the German Emperor,

should sign the treaty .

And why should it not be the same for

all countries that shall participate in the

future peace conference ?

Very sincerely yours

Henri Lambert

An important and able man of Buenos Ayres and

Montevideo, Mr Robert Balmer, to whom I said yesterday that

I foresaw a proposal of "economic peace", coming either from

Europe or from America, told me that such a proposal would

have a very strong and popular support in South-America.

The attitude of Japan is encouraging. I have sent

my "Pax Economica" and written to Viscount Ischii and to

several of these Japanese Gentlemen some weeks ago,

and I please myself in thinking that it may in some

measure have helped for the recent declaration which

~~seems~~ to me to be very unmarkable.

Park Avenue Hotel
32nd & 33rd Streets
New York

4th of october 17

Dear Colonel House,

I have been asking myself which should and could be the guarantees requisite from Germany and her government for the stability and durability of the future treaty of peace.

The « ousting » of the Hohenzollern dynasty seems to me, and probably to some others, to be an « excessive » demand. The adoption of a government responsible to the Parliament is not an easy measure to be carried through ; moreover it would not be a very serious guarantee (in my opinion it is even very questionable whether such a government is a real progress in the Parliamentary system).

I suggest that the necessary guarantee should be this : Germany should have at the peace conference one half of her delegates designated directly by the Reichstag ; these delegates, as well as those designated by the German Emperor, should sign the treaty.

And why should it not be the same for all countries that shall participate in the future peace conference ?

Very sincerely your's,

Henri Lambert

[P.S.]

An important and able man of Buenos Ayres and Montevideo, Mr Robert Balmer, to whom I said yesterday that I foresaw a proposal of « economic peace », coming either from Europe or from America, told me that such a proposal would have a very strong and popular support in South-America.

The attitude of Japan is encouraging. I have sent my « Pax Economica » and written to Viscount Ischii and to several of these Japanese gentlemen some weeks ago, and I please myself in thinking that it may in some measure have helped for the recent declaration – which seems to me to be very remarkable.

Park Avenue Hotel
PARK AVENUE
(FOURTH AVENUE)
32 ND & 33 RD STREETS
FIRE PROOF

FRED. A. REED INC. PROPRIETOR
GEO. C. BROWN, PRESIDENT

JOHN R. MACDONALD MANAGER.
W. P. MERRITT, ASS'T MANAGER

New York 6th of October 17.

Dear Colonel House,

Further reflections have led me to the opinion that the participation of the German people in the Treaty, through a delegation of the Reichstag at the future Conference, would not, by itself and alone, be a sufficient guarantee and that further the „parliamentarization" of the German government is necessary.

This transformation of institutions is a measure questionnable in the case of a Republic — but not in the case of Germany, whatever may be the difficulty of carrying it through during the war and its effect on the prolongation of this.

Very sincerely yours

Henri Lambert

Park Avenue Hotel
32nd & 33rd Streets
New York

6th of October 17

Dear Colonel House,

Further reflections have led me to the opinion that the participation of the German people in the Treaty, through a delegation of the Reichstag at the future conference, would not, by itself and alone, be a sufficient guarantie and that further the « parliamentarization » of the German government is necessary.

This transformation of institutions is a measure questionable in the case of a Republic – but not in the case of Germany, whatever may be the difficulty of carrying it through during the war and its effect on the prolongation of this [war].

Very sincerely your's,

Henri Lambert

Park Avenue Hotel
PARK AVENUE
(FOURTH AVENUE)
32 ND & 33 RD STREETS
FIRE PROOF

~~FRED. A. REED INC., PROPRIETOR~~
GEO. C. BROWN, PRESIDENT

JOHN R. MACDONALD MANAGER.
W. P. MERRITT, ASS'T MANAGER

New York 17th of October 17

Dear Colonel House,

I more and more am under the impression that, if the "Parliamentarization" of the German Government (a reform which, I think, requires a complete reshaping of the constitution of the Empire, with the consent of all its constituent States) were on a fair way of becoming an accomplished fact, a suggestion concerning the composition of the delegations at the peace-conference would be most helpful. This should be, for example, to the effect that the delegation of all and each of the belligerent nations should be comprized of, say, five members, three of whom designated by the Parliaments and two designated by the Governments.

Such a suggestion should be useful from several important points of views (1) it would tend to confer responsibility and prestige to the Parliaments and thus it would favor and hasten "Parliamentarization"; (2) the idea of this composition of delegations would appeal to all peoples and Parliaments (chiefly to the German and Austrian liberals and democrats) and it would incline them all to more eagerly look forward to the conference; (3) the prospect of a successful issue of the conference would be immensely increased by such delegations; (4) the guarantee of a faithful and enduring fulfilment of the Treaty of peace would be the best possible (better than mere democratization of governments, because more directly popular. Very sincerely yours Henri Lambert

Park Avenue Hotel
32nd & 33rd Streets
New York

17th of October 17

Dear Colonel House,

I more and more am under the impression that, <u>if the « Parliamentarization » of the German Government</u> (a reform which, I think, requires a complete reshaping of the constitution of the Empire, with the consent of all its constituent States) <u>were on a fair way of becoming an accomplished fact</u>, a suggestion concerning the composition of the delegations at the peace-conférence would be most helpful. This should be, for example, to the effect that the delegation of all and each of the belligerent nations should be comprized of, say, five members, three of whom designated by the Parliament and two designated by the Governments.

Such a suggestion should be useful from several important points of views ; (1) it would tend to confer responsibility and prestige to the Parliaments and thus it would favor and hasten « Parliamentarization », (2) the idea of this composition of delegations would appeal to all peoples and Parliaments (chiefly to the German and Austrian liberals and democrats) and it would incline them <u>all</u> to more eagerly look forward to the Conference ; (3) The prospect of a successful issue of the Conference would be immensely increased by such delegations ; (4) the guarantee of a faithful and enduring fulfilment of a Treaty of peace would be the best possible (better than mere democratization of government, because <u>more directly</u> popular.

Very sincerely your's,

Henri Lambert

Park Avenue Hotel
PARK AVENUE
(FOURTH AVENUE)
32 ND & 33 RD STREETS
FIRE PROOF

GEORGE C. BROWN.
MANAGING DIRECTOR

New York
8 th of January 1b

Dear Colonel House,

I have taken the liberty of sending the following telegram:

To the President of the United States, Washington

This day, Mr President, will be recorded as that of the greatest, noblest and grandest utterance and act in the history of mankind. Respectfully. Henri Lambert

manufacturer in Charleroi Belgium

I feel, dear Colonel House, that I must complete this admirative expression of appreciation by sending it also to you.

Very sincerely yours

Henri Lambert

Park Avenue Hotel
32nd & 33rd Streets
New York

8th of January 18

Dear Colonel House,

I have taken the liberty of sending the following telegram :
<u>To the President of the United States, Washington.</u>

<u>This day, Mr President, will be recorded as that of the greatest, noblest and grandest utterance* and act in the history of mankind. Respectfully. Henri Lambert. Manufacturer in Charleroi Belgium.</u>

I feel, dear Colonel House, that I must complete this admirative expression of appreciation by sending it also to you.

Very sincerely your's,

Henri Lambert

*P.S. : President Wilson's speech declaration of the famous « Fourteen Points » on which peace was to be based however the third Point – general economic freeing of Trade – which Henri Lambert had so striven for to be the <u>very first</u> Point on which to base the entire peace process was not in first place…

The New Ebbitt

ARMY & NAVY
HEADQUARTERS
WASHINGTON, D.C.,

G. F. SCHUTT, PROPRIETOR.

26th of June 18

Dear Colonel House,

I had to-day, in a general "Shake-hands" reception, the honor to meet the President and took the liberty to handle to him the statement of which copy is enclosed and in which is briefly expressed my opinion on the three main topics of the day.

I am, dear Colonel House, with high regards,

Very sincerely yours

Henri Lambert

The New Ebbitt
Army and Navy
Headquarters
Washington, D.G.

26th of June 18

Dear Colonel House,

I had to-day, in a general « shake-hands » reception, the honor to meet the President and took the liberty, to hand to him the statement of which copy is enclosed and in which is briefly expressed my opinion on the three main topics of the day.

I am dear Colonel House, with high regard, very sincerely your's,

Henri Lambert

Park Avenue Hotel

PARK AVENUE
(FOURTH AVENUE)
32 ND & 33 RD STREETS
FIRE PROOF

GEORGE C. BROWN.
MANAGING DIRECTOR

New York 15th of July 15

1918 ?

Dear Colonel House,

Excuse me to allow myself to suggest that, following the statement of Lord Robert Cecil, the President of the United States, speaking (as announced for some days) on intervention in Russia, is offered the opportunity of anew proposing his „third condition" of the 8th of January and of teaching the world that „clear, plain lesson of fundamental international truth and morality" which is so much needed in all countries, especially in Germany, and which, once understood in the latter country, would within a short time induce, and compel, the German Government to accept the four conditions of the President, as stated in his message of the 4th of of February and the 4ᵗʰ of July.

The economic peace proposal contains in itself the mightiest weapon against the Pan-Germans (especially in their policy toward Russia) as well as against the reactionnairs and revolutionnairs of all other countries. This settlement of the international situation would prepare everywhere the ground for the internal conditions requisite for the really democratic and progressive Solution of the Social question — a Solution that has nothing whatever to do with either the liberal or the Socialistic conceptions and theories — and, of course, still less with the conservative views and aims.

I am, dear Colonel House, with high regards,

Very sincerely yours

Henri Lambert

– Letter 34/1 –

Park Avenue Hotel
32nd & 33rd Streets
New York

15th of July 15 (1918 ?)

Dear Colonel House,

Excuse me to allow myself to suggest that, following the statement of Lord Robert Cecil, the President of the United States, speaking (as announced for some days) on intervention in Russia, is offered the opportunity of anew proposing his « third condition » of the 8th of January and of <u>teaching the world that « clear, plain lesson of fundamental international truth and morality »</u> which is so much needed in all countries, especially in Germany, and which, once understood in the latter country, would within a short time induce, and compel, the German government to accept the <u>fourth</u> condition of the President, as stated in his message of the 4th of February and the 4th of July.

The economic peace proposal contains in itself the mightiest weapon against the Pan-Germans (especially in their policy toward Russia) as well as against the reactionnaries and revolutionnaries of all other countries. This settlement of the international situation would prepare everywhere the ground for the internal conditions requisite for the really democratic and progressive solution of the social question – a solution that has nothing whatever to do with either the liberal or the socialistic conception and theories – and, of course, still less with the conservative views and aims.

I am, dear Colonel House, with high regard, very sincerely your's,

Henri Lambert

Park Avenue Hotel
PARK AVENUE
(FOURTH AVENUE)
32 ND & 33 RD STREETS
FIRE PROOF

FRED. A. REED INC. PROPRIETOR.   JOHN R. MACDONALD MANAGER.

New York 16th of September
18.

Dear Colonel House,

I took the liberty to send you two copies of a recently published lecture which I delivered last April to the Clergy Club of New York. Though, no doubt, the present circumstances make very trying claims on men engaged in, and responsible for, our international policy, I hope that you will find the time necessary for doing me the honor to read this philosophical contribution to the elucidation of the world problem.

In it I have outlined the first rational and scientific explanation ever given (or attempted, at least) of the formation of the human soul. With a good deal of supplementary purely scientific arguments — physical, chemical and biological — this theory will constitute a part of a system of general philosophy of which (under the title: "Hypothèse sur l'Evolution physique et métaphysique de l'Energie") I am preparing the exposition, and which, I hope, will mark a serious step toward the necessary reconciliation of science and religion, Darwinism and Christianity. This general philosophy will form an ensemble with my conception of the solution of the social problem and with that of the settlement of the international problem.

Referring to the present Austrian peace move, allow me to again express and to confirm my opinion that President Wilson's "third condition" of the 8th of January 1918, offers and will continue to offer, the only possible ground of international understanding. So long as Germany and Austria (as well as the other belligerents) do not realize and grasp this, there will be no use in proposing or accepting peace meetings; for, these, of necessity, would firstly and mainly be concerned with territorial, colonial, or nationalistic readjustments and there does not exist the least prospect or possibility of success in negotiations thus initiated and conducted.

The world can be saved from this war and its consequences (much graver than the war itself) only through the general recognition of a new truth — that of the duty of all nations and all men to cooperate in freedom of exchange and in equality of rights to the opportunities afforded by Nature (i.e. the Earth's land, seas, water ways and atmosphere) only on this natural basis, of general economic freedom and equality of rights, can the necessary international and social institutions and organizations be established with any chance of successful working and of durability (the necessary "machineries" being, in the international realm: the league of nations, with self-government of nationalities in independence or autonomy; and in the social realm: a new organization of universal suffrage and an equally new organization of the right of cooperation or association)

If the basic "third condition" of the President of the United States is considered impossible of attainment, or inacceptable, then the inescapable outcome and end of the present tragedy is a general falling back of Mankind into barbarity. (in process in Russia) — A situation, which would be more than grave, might arise if, whilst the allied nations were in great internal difficulties, or in actual anarchy, the Germanic nations and friends were not, because economically oppressed, and could momentarily recombine in view of "liberation".

The greatest peril of the present situation lies in the fact that a very small minority only of the leaders and statesmen have an idea of the real nature of the international and the social problems.

Excuse this indiscreetly long letter and believe me, dear Colonel House, with high regards, very sincerely yours

Henri Lambert

17th of September.
With much gratification I see this morning in the papers the reply of President Wilson to the Austria peace-move.

Park Avenue Hotel
32nd & 33rd Streets
New York

16th of September 18

Dear Colonel House,

I took the liberty to send you two copies of a recently published lecture which I delivered last April to the Clergy Club of New York. Though, no doubt, the present circumstances make very trying claims on men engaged in, and responsible for, our international policy, I hope that you will find the time necessary for doing me the honor to read this philosophical contribution to the elucidation of the world problem.

In it I have outlined the first rational and scientific exploration ever given (or <u>attempted</u>, at least) of the formation of the human soul. With a good deal of supplementary purely scientific arguments, – physical, chemical and biological, – this theory will constitute a part of a system of general philosophy of which (under the title : « Hypothese sur l'Evolution physique et metaphysique de l'Energie »). I am preparing the exposition, and which, I hope, will mark a serious step toward the necessary reconcilation of science and religion, Darwinism and Christianity. This general philosophy will form an ensemble with my conception of the solution of the social problem and with that of the settlement of the international problem.

Referring to the present Austria peace move, allow me to again express and to confirm my opinion that the President Wilson's « third condition, of the 8th of January 1918, offers and will continue to offer, the only possible ground of international understanding. So long as Germany and Austria (as well as the other belligerents) do not realize and grasp this, there will be no use in proposing or accepting peace meetings ; for, these, of necessity, would firstly and mainly be concerned with territorial, colonial, or nationalistic redjustments and there does not exist the least prospect or possibility of success in negotiation thus initiated and conducted.

The world can be saved from this war <u>and its consequences</u> (much graver than the war itself) only through the general recognition of a new truth – that of the <u>duty</u> of all nations and all men to cooperate in freedom of exchange and in equality of rights to the opportunities afforded by Nature (i.e. the earth's land, seas, water ways and atmosphere) only on this natural basis, of general economic freedom and equality of rights, can the necessary international and social institutions and organizations be established with any chance of successful working and of durability (the necessary « machineries » being – in the international realm : the league of nations, with self-government of nationalities in independence or autonomy ; and in the social realm : a new organization of universal suffrage and an equally new organization of the right of cooperation or association).

If the basic « third condition » of the President of the United States is considered impossible of attainment, or inacceptable, then the inescapable outcome and end of the present tragedy is a general falling back of mankind into barbarity (in process in Russia) – a situation, which would be more than grave, might arise if, whilst the allied nations were in great internal difficulties, or in actual anarchy, the Germanic nations and friends <u>were not</u>, because economically oppressed, and could momentarily recombine in view of « liberation ».

The greatest peril of the present situation lies in the fact that a very small minority only, of the leaders and statesmen, have an idea of the real nature of the international and the social problems.

Excuse this indiscreetly long letter and believe me, dear Colonel House, with high regards, very sincerely your's,

Henri Lambert

Park Avenue Hotel
PARK AVENUE
(FOURTH AVENUE)
32 ND & 33 RD STREETS
FIRE PROOF

GEORGE C. BROWN
MANAGING DIRECTOR

New York 3ᵈ of October 18

Dear Colonel House,

I beg to be allowed a brief expression of opinion on present issues.

I. If the new German government were wise — an unlikely supposition — it would announce, first of all, that Germany will be a free trade country after the war.

The time is approaching when universal free trade can, and perhaps must, be proposed as the necessary foundation of a league of nations, of permanent peace, and of the new world order. Circumstances, I suggest, may soon permit, and make it desirable, that immediate absolute free trade be imposed on Germany and Austria as a condition of peace. This would respond (1) to the necessity of securing Great-Britain's assent to the continuation of her free-trade policy (2) to the need of securing the good will of the other belligerent nations (3) to

II.

the utility of removing the very foundation of German economic and military aggressiveness and militancy.

The other belligerent countries would have to accept the principle of free trade, pledging themselves to apply it gradually in such a fashion that they should be absolute free trade within ten years, everyone of these latter countries being left entirely free to choose its own way for achieving this evolution.

As to the non-belligerent nations of the world, there exists no doubt that they would give their assent to this basic condition of a league of nations.

II. Though the President is undoubtedly right in notifying that a league of nations must be in existence at, and for, the final signature of peace, it can be doubted whether this can be completely organized before peace is virtually concluded. I mean that if a preliminary organization, with sufficient detail for being workable, were agreed upon by the United States, Great Britain, France, Italy, Germany and Austria, at a first peace conference, the complete organization could be left to a second conference — which certainly will be necessary for the working out of the solution of the numerous remaining international questions (The first conference could possibly fulfil its task (if properly dealt with) in three weeks; the second possibly not in its three years)

III. Few people see the relationship and necessary connection between the settlement of the international problem and that of the national problems. No international peace can be secured if the peoples forming the league of nations do not live in internal peace and are not able to behave themselves. Therefore the problem of democratic self-government will, immediately after peace, appear to be very urgent. And so, also, naturally, the social problem. In order to avoid <u>everywhere in Europe</u> internal disorder, which might degenerate into anarchy, it will be very important that the question of democratic political organization be solved rapidly (within less than ten years). Up to now democracy is far from having proved to be a real success; before the war the social crisis was not less threatening in democracies than in „autocracies"; and, as to the political crisis, it is cautious not to forget that Parliamentarism <u>everywhere</u> worked less and less satisfactorily. If such was the case with old democracies, what can we expect with young, uneducated, turbulent democracies living amidst the impassioned atmosphere and exceptional difficulties that will long continue to exist as the legacy of war? On this I intend to take the liberty to write you in a few days.

To-day I would like to add on this subject that, if <u>self-government</u> of nationalities (in independence or autonomy according to cases) is an incontestable principle, <u>self-determination</u> perhaps is <u>not</u> such a principle. The formation of the diverse nations and nationalities having not developed as a natural phenomenon and having, in most cases, been the result of an exterior act, it will be required again to have recourse to external action for reshaping the diverse nations of Europe. The principle of self-determination <u>applied now</u> fatally would create a great danger of anarchy. The great urgent need will be to create international stability and security — fundamentally economic — thus making progressively possible the self determination of nationalities as a <u>natural</u> phenomenon. Meanwhile it will be cautious to refrain from too much „reshaping", and autonomy in general will be safer than independence (except for Alsace Lorraine and Poland which could and ought to be made independent States.

With highest regards, I am, dear Colonel House, very sincerely yours

Henri Lambert

Park Avenue Hotel
32nd & 33rd Streets
New York

3rd of October 18

Dear Colonel House,

I beg to be allowed a brief expression of opinion on present issues.

I

If the new German government were wise – an unlikely supposition – it would announce, first of all, than Germany will be a free trade country after the war.

The time is approaching when universal free trade can, and perhaps must, be proposed as the necessary foundation of a league of nations, of permanent peace, and of the new world order. Circumstances, I suggest, may soon permit, and make it desirable, that immediate absolute free trade <u>be imposed on Germany and Austria as a condition of peace</u>. This would respond (1) to the necessity of securing Great-Britain's assent to the continuation of her free-trade policy (2) to the need of securing the good will of the other belligerent nations (3) to the utility of removing the very foundation of German economic and military aggressiveness and militancy.

The other belligerent countries would have to accept <u>the principle</u> of free trade, pledging themselves to apply it gradually in such a fashion that they should be absolute free trade within ten years, every one of these latter countries being <u>left entirely free to choose its own way</u> for achieving this evolution.

As to the non-belligerent nations of the world, there exists no doubt that they would give their assent to this basic condition of a league of nations.

II

Though the President is undoubtedly right in notifying that a league of nations must be in existence at, and for, the <u>final signature</u> of peace, it can be doubted whether this can be completely organized before peace is <u>virtually concluded</u>. I mean that if a preliminary organization, with sufficient detail for being workable, were agreed upon by the United States, Great Britain, France, Italy, Germany and Austria, at a first peace conference, the complete organization could be left to a second conference – which certainly will be necessary for the working out of the solution of numerous remaining international questions. (The first conference could possibly fulfil its task (if properly dealt with) in three weeks ; the second possibly not in its first three years).

III

Few people see the relationship and necessary connection between the settlement of the international probem and that of the national problems. No international peace can be secured if the peoples forming the league of nations do not live in internal peace and are not able to behave themselves. Therefore the problem of democratic self-government will, immediately after peace, appear to be very urgent. And so, also, naturally, the social problem. In order to avoid <u>everywhere in Europe</u> internal disorder, which might degenerate into anarchy, it will be very important that the question of democratic political organization be solved rapidly (within less than ten years). Up to now democracy is far from having proved to be a real success ; before the war the social crisis was not less threatening in democracies than in « autocracies », as to the political crisis, it is cautious not to forget that Parliamentarism <u>everywhere</u> worked less and less satisfactorily. If such was the case with old democracies, what can we expect with young, uneducated, turbulent democraties living amidst the impassioned atmosphere and exceptional difficulties that will long continue to exist as the legacy of war ? On this I intend to take the liberty to write you in a few days.

To-day I would like to add on this suject that, if <u>self government</u> of nationalities (in independence or autonomy according to cases) is an incontestable principle, <u>self-determination</u> perhaps is <u>not</u> such a principle. The formation of the diverse nations and nationalities not having developed as a natural phenomenon and having, in most cases, been the result of an exterior act, it will be required again to have recourse to external action for reshaping the diverse nations of Europe. The principle of self-determination <u>applied now</u> fatally would create a great danger of anarchy. The great urgent need will be to create international stability and security – fundamentally economic – thus making progressively possible the self determination of nationalities <u>as a natural phenomenon</u>. Meanwhile it will be cautions to refrain from too much « reshaping », and autonomy in general will be safer than independence (except for Alsace Lorraine and Poland which could and might to be made independent States.

With highest regards, I am, dear Colonel House, very sincerely your's,

Henri Lambert

President Woodrow Wilson (1856-1924).

Park Avenue Hotel
PARK AVENUE
(FOURTH AVENUE)
32 ND & 33 RD STREETS
FIRE PROOF

GEORGE C. BROWN
MANAGING DIRECTOR

New York

Dear Colonel House,

Referring to the suggestion which I have taken the liberty to make, I would like to add that, if the Kaiser did not accept that the Reichstag be substituted for him in the peace proposal, it is most likely that Austria and Turkey would desert their allies.

The "unconditional acceptance" of the Fourteen Points may be a little too radical. If the Reichstag had observations to present they should be specified and justified.

Very sincerely yours

Henri Lambert

7½ of Oct. 1918

Park Avenue Hotel
32nd & 33rd Streets
New York

7th of October 1918

Dear Colonel House,

Refering to the suggestion which I have taken the liberty to make, I would like to add that, if the Kaiser did not accept that the Reichstag be substituted for him in the peace proposal, it is most likely that Austria and Turkey would desert their ally.

The « inconditional acceptance » of the Fourteen Points may be a little too radical. If the Reichstag had observations to present they should be specified and justified.

Very sincerely your's,

Henri Lambert

TELEGRAM.

The White House,

Washington.

12UNIMMA 35

New York, Oct. 7,1918.

Colonel House,
        Washington,D.C.

   Take liberty suggest that United States answer that they decline
consider proposal unless it be the direct specific outcome of a new vote
by the Reichstag the proposal should include unconditional acceptance of
fourteen conditions.

                        Lambert.

Telegram

The White House
Washington

New York, Oct. 7 1918

Colonel House,

Washington, D.C.

Take liberty suggest that United states answer that they decline consider proposal unless it be the direct specific outcome of a new vote by the Reichstag the proposal should include unconditional acceptance of fourteen conditions.

Lambert.

CABLE ADDRESS "PARK AVENUE"
W. U. COD

Park Avenue Hotel

PARK AVENUE
(FOURTH AVENUE)
32 ND & 33 RD STREETS
FIRE PROOF

FRED. A. REED INC., PROPRIETOR.

GEORGE C. BROWN,
MANAGING DIRECTOR

New York

Dear Colonel House,

Allow me a suggestion.

I would answer that the United States will consider peace only if it is proposed as the direct and specific outcome of a new vote of the German Reichstag. The proposal must include unconditional acceptance of the Fourteen Conditions of January 8th 1918.

Very sincerely yours

Henri Lambert

7th of October 18.

P.S. The new vote would instruct us as to the real state of mind in Germany; it would leave no doubt to the German nation, and the outside world, as to the surrender of the German militarists; it would give much prestige to the Reichstag if this chooses.—

Park Avenue Hotel
32nd & 33rd Streets
New York

7th of October 18

Dear Colonel House,

Allow me a suggestion.

I would answer that the United States will consider peace only if it is proposed as the direct and specific outcome of a <u>new vote</u> of the German Reichstag. The proposal must include unconditional acceptance of the Fourteen Conditions of January 8th 1918.

Very sincerely your's,

Henri Lambert

P.S. The new vote would instruct us as to the real state of mind in Germany ; it would leave no doubt to the German nation, and the outside world, as to the surrender of the German militarists ; it would give much prestige to the Reichstag if this chooses.

Park Avenue Hotel. Writing room.

Park Avenue Hotel
PARK AVENUE
(FOURTH AVENUE)
32 ND & 33 RD STREETS
FIRE PROOF

GEORGE C. BROWN,
MANAGING DIRECTOR

New York, 11th of Oct. 18.

Dear Colonel House,

It is not improbable that the German Government will submit its answer to the Reichstag before sending it. This could only happen if the answer were an unconditional acceptance of the "Fourteen Points"; for, the German Government would not take the risk of submitting to the Reichstag a "conditional acceptance".

If the German answer is not first submitted to the Reichstag, two cases are possible: (1) the answer is conditional, case in which I am more than strongly inclined to think that it should be flatly rejected by the United States' Government; (2) the answer is unconditional acceptance, case in which I could not enough advocate,

— if this were necessary — that the United States should demand <u>a vote</u> by the Reichstag.

This being done, four possibilities exist :

A.— <u>The Kaiser rejects the demand and the Reichstag favor it.</u> — This would provoke intense political strife within the nation, great discontent in the army, and possibly revolution — probably <u>ultimate</u> revolution. It would have as its consequence the desertion by Austria and Turkey of their ally.

B.— <u>The Kaiser accepts to comply to the demand as well as does the Reichstag.</u> — This would, in the eyes of the German people, and of the whole world, signify surrender of the militarists and the army to the civilian power. It would confer great prestige on the Reichstag and ensure the political democratization of Germany.

C.— <u>Both the Kaiser and the Reichstag refuse to comply to the U.S. demand.</u> — Highly improbable; but would show us unmistakably that the end of the war in a satisfactory way is possible only through unconditional <u>military</u> surrender.

D.— <u>The Kaiser accepts and the Reichstag rejects.</u> — So improbable that it does not require any present consideration.

———

In the huge game of chess that is going on,

Park Avenue Hotel

PARK AVENUE
(FOURTH AVENUE)
32ND & 33RD STREETS
FIRE PROOF

GEORGE C. BROWN,
MANAGING DIRECTOR

New York

II

and which is to settle for ever the fate of all nations of the Earth, the situation clearly appears to me to be the following : two moves are indicated, each of which is entirely safeguarded and practically certain as to its results; they are final. The first puts an end to Kaiserism, and to the German Empire as such. The second move solves the world problem in its international bearings, and prepares the necessary condition for its certain solution in its national aspects and bearings.

First move : Demand by the United States of a Reichstag vote on the unconditional acceptance of the Fourteen Points. — The vote necessarily would be preceded by a discussion which would (1) give us every desirable and even every possible enlightenment as to the state of mind of the German nation; (2) establish the responsibilities among the various parties and political personalities in Germany; (3) throw the burden of a great part of the work of the eventual peace conference on the German Reichstag.

The vote itself would give us absolute security as to the outcome of the eventual peace conference; for dishonesty at this conference would find the great majority of the German people and army hostile and would leave Germany incapable of pursuing the war.

<u>Second move</u>: Imposition on Germany, Austria, Bulgaria and Turkey of immediate absolute Free Trade.

This would (1) destroy and abolish the very foundation of German economic and military aggressiveness and militancy; (2) eliminate practically all questions and issues of internal or national policy concerned with protection and free-trade, in the United States, Great Britain, in France, Italy; (3) remove purely and simply the Brest-Litovsk and Bucharest treaties; (4) introduce universal free trade; (5) provide the basis of a league of nations; (6) secure permanent peace; (7) provide the necessary <u>conditions and basis for the solution of the social and political crisis in all nations.</u>

I mean, of course, that the "two moves" should take place before any acceptance of a peace conference, that is to say, that the second "move" should immediately follow the vote by the Reichstag and be concomitant with the acknowledgment of receipt# of the notification by Germany of such vote.

With highest regards, very sincerely yours

Henri Lambert

by the United States

Park Avenue Hotel
32nd & 33rd Streets
New York

11th of October 18

Dear Colonel House,

It is not improbable that the German government will submit its answer to the Reichstag before sending it. This could only happen if the answer were an unconditional acceptance of the « Fourteen Points » ; for, the German Government would not take the risk of submitting to the Reichstag a « conditional acceptance ».

If the German answer <u>is</u> <u>not</u> first submitted to the Reichstag, two cases are possible : (1) the answer is conditional, case in which I am more than strongly inclined to think that it should be flatly rejected by the United States governent ; (2) the answer is <u>un</u>conditional acceptance, case in which I could not enough advocate, - if this were necessary – that the United States should <u>demand a vote</u> by the Reichstag.

This being done, four possibilities exist :

A.   <u>The Kaiser rejects the demand and the Reichstag favor it</u>. This would provoke intense political strife within the nation, great discontent in the army, and possibly revolution – probably <u>ultimate</u> revolution. It would have as its consequence the desertion by Austria and Turkey of their ally.

B.   <u>The Kaiser accepts to comply to the demand as well as does the Reichstag</u>. – This would, in the eyes of the German people, and of the whole world, signify surrender of the militarists and the army to the civilian power. It would confer great prestige on the Reichstag and ensure the political democratization of Germany.

C.   <u>Both the Kaiser and the Reichstag refuse to comply to the U.S. demand</u>. – Highly improbable ; but would show us unmistakably that the end of the war in a satisfactory way is possible only through unconditional <u>military</u> surrender.

D.   <u>The Kaiser accepts and the Reichstag rejects</u>. – So improbable that it does not require any present consideration.

————

In the huge game of chess that is going on,

II

and which is to settle forever the fate of all nations of the Earth, the situation clearly appears to me to be the following ; two moves are indicated, each of which is entirely safeguarded and practically certain as to its results ; they are final. The first puts an end to Kaiserisme, and to the German Empire as such. The second move solves the world problem in its international bearings, and prepares the necessary condition for its <u>certain solution</u> in its <u>national</u> aspects and bearings.

<u>First move</u> : <u>demand by the United States of a Reichstag vote on the unconditional acceptance of the Fourteen Points</u>. The vote necessarily would be preceded by a discussion which would (1) give us every desirable and even every possible enlightenment as to the state of mind of the German nation ; (2) establish the responsibilities among the various parties and political personalities in Germany ; (3) throw the burden of a great part of the work of the eventual peace conference on the German Reichstag.

The vote itself would give us absolute security as to the outcome of the eventual peace conference ; for dishonesty at this conference would find the great majority of the German people and army hostile and would leave Germany incapable of pursuing the war.

<u>Second move</u> : <u>Imposition on Germany, Austria, Bulgaria and Turquey of immediate absolute Free Trade</u>. This would (1) destroy and abolish the very foundation of German economic and military aggressiveness and militancy ; (2) elimination practically all questions and issues of internal or national policy concerned with protection and free-trade, in the United states, great Britain, France, Italy ; (3) remove purely and simply the Brest-Litovsk and Bucharest treaties ; (4) introduce universal free trade ; (5) provide the basis of a league of nations ; (6) secure permanent peace ; (7) <u>proside the necessary condition and basis for the solution of the social and political crisis in all nations</u>.

I mean, of course, that the « two moves » should take place before any acceptance of a peace conference, that is to say, that the second « move » should immmediately follow the vote by the Reichstag and be concomitant with the acknowledgment of receipt* of the notification by Germany of such vote.

*by the United States.

With highest regard, very sincerely your's,

Henri Lambert

Park Avenue Hotel

PARK AVENUE
(FOURTH AVENUE)
32 ND & 33 RD STREETS

FIRE PROOF

GEORGE C. BROWN,
MANAGING DIRECTOR

New York

13 th of October 18

Dear Colonel House,

The present day is the most solemn in the history of mankind — past and future. If the <u>two moves</u> are made — the second immediately following the first — the world is saved, internationally <u>and socially</u>. If they are not made, <u>nothing</u> is secured

Very sincerely yours

Henri Lambert

For men who have insight, and who do not allow themselves to be brutalized in their views and acts, the best imaginable guarantee for the evacuation and the armistice appears to be in the <u>vote by the Reichstag</u>.

Park Avenue Hotel
32nd & 33rd Streets
New York

13th of October 18

Dear Colonel House,

The present day is the most solemn in the history of mankind-past and futur. If the <u>two moves</u> are made – the second immediately following the first – the world is saved, internationaly <u>and socially</u>. If they are not made, <u>nothing</u> is secured.

For men who have insight, and who do not allow themselves to be brutalized in their views and acts, the best imaginable for the evacuation and the armistice appears to be in <u>the vote by the Reichstag</u>.

Very sincerely your's,

Henri Lambert

CABLE ADDRESS "PARK AVENUE"
W. U. CODE.

Park Avenue Hotel

PARK AVENUE
(FOURTH AVENUE)
32 ND & 33 RD STREETS
FIRE PROOF

GEORGE C. BROWN,
MANAGING DIRECTOR

New York

13th of October 18

Dear Colonel House,

I very nearly have come to the conclusion, and I allow myself respectfully to suggest to you, that probably the combination of the two moves, into one final "checkmate", is preferable, that is to say, that Germany should be made known that votes by the Reichstag are requested:

(1) on unconditional acceptance of the "14 Points"

(2) on acceptance of immediate absolute free trade for Germany (Austria, Bulgaria and Turkey having to acquiesce for themselves)

before the proposal of armistice can be accepted.

I hesitated on this because the superposition of

the two demands (the 14 Points and free trade) might be considered excessive ; but (1) it does not, in fact, appear more, but _less_, excessive to make simultaneously the two demands than to have them made immediately following one the other; (2) the Reichstag will understand that the acceptance of free trade by Germany is a condition of the acceptance of this by the other nations, and that _only in this way_ can the President of the United States succeed in his undertaking.

Among all belligerent nations, two must be put apart: Germany, as the most guilty for the war, and Great Britain, as the least guilty for it. In the interests of the future, and from every point of view, the primary necessity is to reconcile the views and interests of Germany with those of Great Britain; and this is possible, and desirable _and just_, only through the acceptance by Germany of Great-Britain's ideas and policy — firstly and fundamentally, Great-Britain's _economic_ ideas and policy: free trade.

This being done, the ground is cut under the feet of the Protectionists not only in England but in the whole World (the United States included.)

There are only two peaces: the free trade peace, and the peace that is not free trade. The latter, which fundamentally would be an _undemocratic peace_, would leave the world in a situation much worse than before the war, both internationally and socially. The former, the economic peace, which fundamentally is the democratic peace, saves everything — internationally and _socially_. On this fundamental democratic peace will be built the international and _social_ "machineries" which are necessary, _and which will save the world_.

Very sincerely yours

Henri Lambert

Park Avenue Hotel
32nd & 33rd Streets
New York

13th of October 18

Dear Colonel House,

I very nearly have come to the conclusion, and I allow myself respectfully to suggest to you, that probably the combination of the two moves, <u>into one final « checkmate »</u> is preferable, that is to say, that Germany should be made known that votes by the Reichstag are requested :

(1)   On unconditional acceptance of the « 14 Points »

(2)   On acceptance of immediate absolute free trade for Germany (Austria, Bulgaria and Turkey having to acquiesce for themselves).

Before the proposal of armistice can be accepted.

I hesitated on this because the superposition of the two demands (the 14 Points <u>and</u> free trade) might be considered excessive ; but (1) it does not, in fact, appear more, <u>but</u> <u>less</u>, excessive to make simultanconsly the two demands than to have them made immediately following one the other ; (2) the Reichstag will understand that the acceptance of free trade by German is a condition of the acceptance of this by the other nations, and that <u>only in this way</u> can the President of the United States succeed in his undertaking.

Among all belligerent nations, two must be put apart : Germany, as the most guilty for the war, and Great Britain, as the least guilty for it. In the interests of the future, and from every point of view, the primary necessity is to reconcile the views and interests of Germany with those of Great Britain ; and this is possible, and desirable, <u>and first</u>, only through the acceptance by Germany of Great Britain's ideas and policy – firstly and fundamentally Great Britain's <u>economic</u> ideas and policy : <u>free trade</u>.

This being done, the ground is cut under the feet of the Protectionists not only in England but in the whole world (the United states included).

There are only two peaces : the free trade peace, and the peace that is <u>not</u> free trade. The latter, which fundamentally would be an <u>un</u>democratic peace, would have the world in a situation much worse than before the war, both internationally us socially. The former, the economic peace, which fundamentally is the democratic peace, secures everything – internationally and <u>socially</u>. On this fundamental democratic peace will be built the international <u>and social</u> « machineries » which are necessary, <u>and which will save the world</u>.

Very sincerely your's,

Henri Lambert

V

Paris "Peace Conference" and Versailles Treaty

Paris, March 22, 1919.

Dear Mr. Lambert:

Your letter of March 14th
with its enclosure has just come to me and
I have read them both with profit and pleasure.

Sincerely yours,

Henri Lambert Esq.
     Charleroi,
          BELGIUM.

Paris, March 22, 1919

Dear Mr Lambert :

Your letter of March 16th with its enclosure has just come to me and I have read then both with profit and pleasure.

Sincerely your's,

[House]

Henri Lambert Esq.
Charleroi
BELGIUM.

HENRI LAMBERT

INGÉNIEUR

CHARLEROI

Charleroi, March 16th
1919.

Dear Colonel House,

It appears every day
more and more clearly that freedom
of international economic intercourse
offers the sole alternative for increasing
territorial ambitions and greed, for
conquests and annexations, and that
a "Pax Economica" is the only conclusive
settlement of the problem confronting the
world, the only possible universal

and permanent peace.

International free exchange and cooperation — gradually to be arrived at — or militarism, imperialism, and wars of increasing gravity — such is the dilemma of mankind's international destinies, eventually ending in barbarity. If the coming treaty of peace is signed without mankind having been taught this great lesson, and having learned this great truth, there will be, in an immediate future, for the world even less security than there was in the past, and a combined social and international cataclysm, more terrific and graver than that we have gone through, is unavoidable,

possibly to take place before ten years.
For this decisive catastrophe, those who
have the actual Knowledge of the solving
and saving principle of fundamental
liberty and Justice, and have failed to
proclaim it in this fateful emergency,
will be held responsible by future generations, by history, and before God.

In a recent book entitled "The
only possible Peace", Fredric C. Howe
concludes to the necessity of a "Pax
Economica". I take the liberty to enclose
a copy of The Public reproducing Howe's
chapter. This article, allow me to
suggest, is worth reading. I would
only say, in addition to its content,
that if "the peace which is to come
must be a 'Pax Economica'", the cornerstone

of such a peace, as well as of a democratized world, must be a free trade Germany. The Article First of the coming peace treaty should be:

"The German Zollverein is abolished for ever. Free Trade is to be put into practice between the German States as well as between these and the whole outside World, i.e., without any customs restrictions on the part of Germany.

"Germany in turn will be admitted in the League of Nations and granted equality of trade conditions everywhere in the world — the conditions of this being: (1) a free trade Germany; (2) a Germany paying just and adequate indemnities for the destructions caused by the war in the countries invaded by her armies."

Believe me, dear Colonel House,
With high regards
Very faithfully yours
Henri Lambert

HENRI LAMBERT
Ingénieur
CHARLEROI

March 16th 1919

Dear Colonel house,

It appears every day more and more clearly that freedom of international economic intercourse offers the sole alternative for increasing territorial ambition and greed, for conquests and annexations, and that a « Pax Economica » is the only conclusion settlement of the problem confronting the world, the only possible universal and permanent peace.

International free exchange and cooperation – gradually to be arrived at – or militarisme, imperialisme, and wars of increasing gravity – such is the dilemma of mankind's international destinies, eventually ending in barbarity. If the coming treaty of peace is signed without mankind having been taught this great lesson, and having learned this great truth, there will be, in an immediate future, for the world even less security than there was in the past and a <u>combined social and international</u> cataclysm, more terrific and graver than that we have gone through, is unavoidable, possibly to take place before ten years. For this decisive catastrophe, those who have the actual knowledge of the solving and saving principle of fundamental liberty, and justice, and have failed to proclaim it in this fateful emergency, will be held responsible by future generations, by history, and before God.

In a recent book entitled « The only possible Peace » Frederic C. Have concludes to the necessity of a « Pax Economica ». I take the liberty to enclose a copy of <u>The Public</u> reproducing Howe's chapter. This article, allow me to suggest, is worth reading. I would only say, in addition to its content, that if « the peace which is to come must be a « Pax Economica », the cornerstone of such a peace, as well as of a democratized world, must be <u>a free trade Germany</u>. The Article First of the coming peace treaty should be : <u>The German Zollverein is abolished for ever. Free Trade is to be put into practice between the German States as well as between these and the whole outside world, i.e., without any customs restrictions on the part of Germany.</u>

« Germany <u>in turn will be admitted in the League of Nations and granted equality of trade conditions everywhere in the world – the conditions of this being : (1) a free trade Germany ; (2) a Germany paying just and adequate indemnities for the destructions caused by the war in the countries invaded by her armies</u> ».

Believe me, dear Colonel House, with high regards, very faithfully your's,

Henri Lambert

HENRI LAMBERT
INGÉNIEUR
CHARLEROI

11 - IV / 19

Dear Colonel House,

I take the liberty to send you two copies of the Gazette de Charleroi reproducing a letter which I have contributed to the

Nieuwe Rotterdamsche Courant

and which appeared in this paper on the 5th of the present month.

With high regards, I am,

very sincerely yours

Henri Lambert

– Letter 45/1 –

HENRI LAMBERT
INGENIEUR
CHARLEROI

11-IV-19

Dear Colonel House,

I take the liberty to send you two copies of the <u>Gazette de Charleroi</u> reproducing a letter which I have contributed ot the <u>Nieuwe Rotterdamsche Courant</u> and which appeared in this paper on the 8th of the present month.

With high regards, I am very sincerely your's,

Henri Lambert

HENRI LAMBERT

INGÉNIEUR

CHARLEROI

Article Premier :

> Les douanes du Zollverein sont abolies.
> — Le libre-échange reste établi entre les
> Etats de l'Allemagne et celle-ci ne pourra
> opposer au commerce extérieur aucune
> restriction douanière.— Les autres nations
> adoptent le libre-échange en principe ;
> elles s'engagent à le mettre graduelle-
> ment, en pratique au cours des 20 prochai-
> nes années, par les voies et moyens qu'elles
> jugeront les mieux appropriés.
> L'Allemagne sera admise dans la Société
> des Nations et jouira, sur tous les marchés
> du monde, du traitement de la nation la
> plus favorisée, à la condition qu'elle s'en-
> gage à s'acquitter de justes indemnités
> réparatrices des dommages causés par sa
> guerre.

Comment concevoir que toutes les jeunes républiques de l'Europe centrale et orientale puissent vivre en paix — ou, même, qu'elles puissent vivre — s'il n'est pas stipulé dans le Traité de paix qu'elles devront pratiquer entre elles la liberté des échanges ?

Cette liberté ne constitue-t-elle pas, d'ailleurs, le fondement commun nécessaire pour toutes les démocraties ?

HENRI LAMBERT
Ingénieur
CHARLEROI

Article Premier :

LES DOUANES DU SOLLVEREIN SONT ABOLIES – LE LIBRE-ÉCHANGE RESTE ETABLI ENTRE LES ÉTATS DE L'ALLEMAGNE ET CELLE-CI NE POURRA OPPOSER AU COMMERCE EXTÉRIEUR AUCUNE RESTRICTION DOUANIÈRE – <u>LES AUTRES NATIONS ADOPTENT LE LIBRE-ÉCHANGE EN PRINCIPE ; ELLES S'ENGAGENT À LE METTRE, GRADUELLEMENT EN PRATIQUE AU COURS DES 20 PROCHAINES ANNÉES, PAR LES VOIES ET MOYENS QU'ELLES JUGERONT LES MIEUX APPROPRIÉS.</u>

L'ALLEMAGNE SERA ADMISE DANS LA SOCIÉTE DES NATIONS ET JOUIRA, SUR TOUS LES MARCHÉS DU MONDE, DU TRAITEMENT DE LA NATION LA PLUS FAVORISÉE, À LA CONDITION QU'ELLE S'ENGAGE À S'ACQUITTER DE JUSTES INDEMNITÉS RÉPARATRICES DES DOMMA-GES CAUSÉS PAR SA GUERRE.

Comment concevoir que toutes les jeunes républiques de l'Europe centrale et orientale puissent vivre en paix – ou, même, qu'<u>elles puissent vivre</u> – s'il n'est pas stipulé dans le traité de paix qu'elles devront pratiquer entre elles la liberté des échanges ?

Cette liberté ne constitue-t-elle pas, d'ailleurs, le fondement commun nécessaire pour <u>toutes</u> les démocraties ?

HENRI LAMBERT
Ingénieur
CHARLEROI

(Capitals indicate newspaper clipping pasted on correspondence card; balance in Lambert's handwriting:)

Article Premier:

LES DOUANES DU ZOLLVEREIN SONT ABOLIES - LE LIBRE-
ÉCHANGE RESTE ÉTABLI ENTRE LES ETATS DE L'ALLEMAGNE ET
CELLE-CI NE POURRA OPPOSER AU COMMERCE EXTÉRIEUR AUCUNE
RESTRICTION DOUANIÈRE - LES AUTRES NATIONS ADOPTENT LE
LIBRE-ÉCHANGE EN PRINCIPE; ELLES S'ENGAGENT À LE METTRE,
GRADUELLEMENT, EN PRATIQUE AU COURS DES 20 PROCHAINES
ANNÉES, PAR LES VOIES ET MOUENS QU'ELLES JUGERONT LES
MIEUX APPROPRIES

L'ALLEMAGNE SERA ADMISE DANS LA SOCIÉTÉ DES NATIONS ET
JOUIRA, SUR TOUS LES MARCHÉS DU MONDE, DU TRAITEMENT DE LA
NATION LA PLUS FAVORISÉE, À LA CONDITION QU'ELLE S'ENGAGE
À S'ACQUITTER DE JUSTES INDEMNITÉS RÉPARATRICES DES DOM-
MAGES CAUSÉS PAR SA GUERRE

Comment concevoir que toutes les jeunes républiques de
l'Europe centrale et orientale puissent vivre en paix - ou,
même, qu'elles puissent vivre - s'il n'est pas stipulé dans
le traité de paix qu'elles devront pratiquer entre elles la
liberté des échanges?

Cette liberté ne constitue-t*elle pas, d'ailleurs, le
fondement commun nécessaire pour toutes les démocraties?

– Lettre 45/4 –

HENRI LAMBERT
Ingénieur
CHARLEROI

Capitals indicate newspaper clipping pasted on correspondence card ;
balance in Lambert's handwriting :

<u>Article Premier</u> :

LES DOUANES DU SOLLVEREIN SONT ABOLIES – LE LIBRE-
ÉCHANGE RESTE ÉTABLI ENTRE LES ÉTATS DE L'ALLEMAGNE ET CELLE-
CI NE POURRA OPPOSER AU COMMERCE EXTÉRIEUR AUCUNE
RESTRICTION DOUANIÈRE – <u>LES AUTRES NATIONS ADOPTENT LE
LIBRE-ÉCHANGE EN PRINCIPE ; ELLES S'ENGAGENT À LE METTRE,
GRADUELLEMENT, EN PRATIQUE AU COURS DES 20 PROCHAINES
ANNÉES, PAR LES VOIES ET MOYENS QU'ELLES JUGERONT LES MIEUX
APPROPRIÉS.</u>

L'ALLEMAGNE SERA ADMISE DANS LA SOCIÉTE DES NATIONS ET
JOUIRA, SUR TOUS LES MARCHÉS DU MONDE, DU TRAITEMENT DE LA
NATION LA PLUS FAVORISÉE, À LA CONDITION QU'ELLE S'ENGAGE
À S'ACQUITTER DE JUSTES INDEMNITÉS RÉPARATRICES DES DOMMA-
GES CAUSÉS PAR SA GUERRE.

Comment concevoir que toutes les jeunes républiques de l'Europe
centrale et orientale puissent vivre en paix – ou, même, qu'<u>elles puissent
vivre</u> – s'il n'est pas stipulé dans le traité de paix qu'elles devront pratiquer
entre elles la liberté des échanges ?

Cette liberté ne constitue-t-elle pas, d'ailleurs, le fondement commun nécessaire pour <u>toutes</u> les démocraties ?

HENRI LAMBERT

INGÉNIEUR

CHARLEROI

26/IV/19.

Dear Colonel House,

Excuse me again to address you in order (if needed) to impress on you the idea of the usefulness, of the necessity, of making Germany a free trade country and, thus, the cornerstone of European international democracy.

The German peace delegation to Paris, most probably, if they have the least diplomatic skill, with the least intelligence of truth, justice and progress, will insist on the application of President Wilson's "third point". They will rightly claim everywhere in the world a "most favored nation's treatment". This should be granted to them. But not unconditionally.

Firstly, and before all, Germany of course

must pledge herself to pay just and adequate indemnities for the damages caused by the war in the countries *or regions* invaded by her armies.

The "third point" reads : " The removal, so far as possible, of all economic barriers, and an equality of trade conditions among all nations consenting to peace and associating themselves for its maintenance "

Now, the "removal, so far as possible, of all economic barriers.." can, in entire truth, sincerity, honesty and justice, be interpreted as meaning that all custom's barriers can and must immediately be removed in Germany, but cannot be removed immediately in the other countries, which however can and will remove them gradually, say in 20 years, through their own ways and means.

Moreover, Germany is not entitled to claim for her goods the continuation of free admittance in Great Britain and the British crown dominions,

if she herself refuses to adopt the British free trade
system and policy. And this will be preserved
by Great-Britain, and adopted by the other countries
in the world, <u>only if</u> Germany herself becomes,
immediately and unconditionally, free trade. This,
if not offered by Germany should be imposed on her,
in answer to her claims for equality of economic rights.
No more powerful argument could be furnished
to the British free traders.

Germany becoming <u>immediately</u>, and
the other countries agreeing to become <u>gradually</u>,
free trade, there will exist no reason, no obstacle,
no excuse, against granting Germany in the
whole world the most favored nation's treatment
i.e. « an equality of trade conditions » as expressed
in the "third point", <u>together with her admittance
in the Society of Nations.</u>

Thus, the "association" of the nations, for the
maintenance of peace, founded on equality of economic
rights and on fundamental justice, would be a real
<u>Society</u> — not a <u>League</u>, not a coalition

of brutal forces, as must inescapably be a combination of nations in order to secure inequality of the basic economic rights, i.e. economic privileges and monopolies.

In short, the "third point" supposes and requires an immediate free trade Germany, and a gradually free trade becoming world, as the realistic basis of a true "association" of nations for the maintenance of peace.

War always had (and we now clearly see that it would continue to have) conquest of territory, extension of domination, increase of power, as its main motive and purpose. War, of course, cannot disappear except through the removal of its cause — the desire for, interest in, necessity of, more territory, domination, power. Such removal is possible only through the (immediate or gradual) throwing open of the world to the free general intercourse, equal economic rights and opportunities of mankind — that will give contentment to all earth's peoples. Such is the natural and necessary process for maintaining peace among nations.

With high regards, I am, dear Colonel House, Very sincerely yours

Henri Lambert

190

HENRI LAMBERT
Ingénieur
CHARLEROI

26/4/19

Dear Colonel House,

Excuse me again to address you in order (if needed) to impress on you the idea of the usefulness, <u>of the necessity</u>, of making Germany a free trade country and, thus, the cornerstone of European international democracy.

The German peace delegation to Paris, most probably, if they have the least diplomatic skill, with the least intelligence of truth, justice and progress, will insist on the application of President Wilson's « third point ». They will rightly claim everywhere in the world a « most favored nation's treatment ». This should be granted to them. <u>But not unconditionally</u>.

Firstly, and before all, Germany of course must pledge herself to pay just and adequate indemnities for the damages caused by the war <u>in the countries or regions invaded by her armies</u>.

The « third point » reads : « The removal, <u>so far as possible</u>, of all economic barriers, and an equality of trade conditions among all nations consenting to peace and associating themselves for its maintenance ».

Now, the « removal, <u>so far as possible</u>, of all economic barriers… » can, in entire truth, sincerity, honesty and justice, be interpreted as meaning that all custom's barriers can and must <u>immediately</u> be removed in Germany, but <u>cannot</u> be removed immediately in the other countries, which however <u>can</u> and <u>will</u> remove them gradually, say in 20 years, through their own ways and means.

Moreover, Germany is not entitled to claim for her goods the continuation of free admittance in Great Britain and the British crown dominions, if she herself refuses to adopt the British free trade system and policy.

And this will be preserved by Great-Britain, and adopted by the other countries in the world, <u>only if</u> Germany herself becomes, immediately and unconditionally, free trade. This, if not offered by Germany should be imposed on her, in answer to her claims for equality of economic rights. No more powerful argument could be furnisher to the British free traders.

Germany becoming <u>immediately</u>, and the other countries aprecing to become <u>gradually</u> free trade, there will exist no reason, no obstacle, no excuse, against granting Germany in the whole word the most favored nations treatment, i.e. « an equality of trade conditions » as represent in the « third point », <u>together with her admittance in the Society of Nations</u>.

Thus the « associations », of the nations, for the maintenance of peace, founded on aquality of economic rights and on fundamental justice, would be a real <u>Society</u> not a <u>League</u>, not a coalition of brutal forces, as must inescapably be a combination of nations in order to secure inequality of the basic economic rights, i.e. economic privileges and monopolies.

In short, the « third point » supposes and requires an immediate free trade Germany, and a gradually free trade becoming world, as the realistic basis of a true « association » of nations for the maintenance of peace.

War always had (and we now clearly see that it would continue to have) conquest of territory, extension of domination, increase of power, as its main motive and purpose. War, of course, cannot disappear except through the removal of its cause – the desire for, interest in, necessity of, more territory, domination, power, such removal is possible only through the (immediate or gradual) throwing open of the world to the force general intercourse, equal economic rights and opportunities of mankind – that will give contentment to all earth's people. Such is the natural and necessary process for maintening peace among nations.

With high regard, I am, dear Colonel House, very sincerely your's,

Henri Lambert

VI

Final correspondence :
"… immensely regretful …"

Hôtel Astoria
Bruxelles

25th of December 32

Dear Colonel House,

I have just cut from "Le Peuple" (Belgian main Socialistic newspaper) the inclosed article, whose content incites me to send you two recent pamphlets. They will show you that, since 1918, I have persisted in my propaganda for a "Pax Economica". But I feel compelled to add that politicians, "intellectuals" and "men-in-the-street" are not more receptive to simple concepts and truths in Europe than in America (they might even be somewhat less, as you may have observed)

The greatest and possibly irremediable peril in the present historic conjunctures is, in my opinion, not in greediness, egotism, or wickedness of men, but in the visible fact that the intelligence (of rulers as well as ruled) is not at the height nor adequate to the largeness — extending to universality — of the problems confronting humanity and which must be solved (they, moreover, are, when understood, mere questions of common sense) — the only alternative, to their being solved, being a downfall of civilization, consequent to revolution and war (or war and revolution)

It is immensely regretful that President Wilson did not keep firmly, irreducibly, to the "third point": International economic freedom, as first and basic principle of the peace-treaty, would have saved Europe in what concerns international (but not social) # difficulties and dangers.

Yours most sincerely

Henri Lambert

permanent address: Astoria Brussels

Allow me to beg you to read the Appendix II of the pamphlet (with the grey cover). The economic and social problem is, when understood, a question of simple common sense; but it requires, for its being understood, more thinking and also more knowledge than ...

Hôtel Astoria
Bruxelles

25th of December 32

Dear Colonel House,

I have just cut from « Le Peuple » (Belgian main socialistic news-paper) the enclosed article, whose contains incite me to send you two recent pamphlets. They will show you that, since 1918, I have persisted in my propaganda for a « Pax Economica ». But I feel compelled to add that politicians, « intellectuals » and, « men-in-the-street » are not more receptive to simple concepts and truths in Europe than in America (they might even be soon what less, as you may have observed).

The greatest and possibly irremediable peril in the present historic conjunctures is, in my opinion, not in greediness, egotism, or wickedness of men, but in the visible fact that the intelligence (of rulers as well as ruled) is not at the height nor adequate to the largeness – extending, to universality – of the problems confronting humanity and which <u>must</u> be solved (they only alternative to their being solved, being a downfall of civilization, con-sequent to revolution and war (or war and revolution).

It is immensely regretful that President Wilson did not keep firmly, irreductibly, to the « third point ». International economic freedom, as first and basic principle of the peace-treaty, would have saved Europe in what concerns international (but <u>not</u> social)* difficulties and dangers.

Your's most sincerely,

Henri Lambert
Permanent address <u>Astoria Brussels.</u>

*Allow me to beg you to read the appendix II of the pamphlet (with the grey cover). The economic and social problem is, when understood, a question of simple common-sense ; but it requires, for its being understood, more thinking and also more knowledge...

Astoria Hotel, Brussels. © MF. Plissart.

104 East 68th St.
New York.
Jan. 7, 1933.

Dear Mr. Lambert:

Thank you for sending
me the enclosures under cover of your
letter of December 28th.

I very much appreciate your
thinking of me.

With every good wish,

Sincerely yours,

M. Henri Lambert,
Hotel Astoria,
Brussels, Belgium.

104 East 66th St.
New York

Jan. 7, 1933

Dear Mr Lambert,

Thank you for sending me the enclosures under cover of your letter of December 28th.

I very much appreciate your thinking of me.

With every good wish,

Sincerely your's,

Mr Henri Lambert
Hotel Astoria,
Brussels, Belgium

Colonel House and his wife.